Stories from Katrinaland

God Responds to Disaster in New Orleans

MICHAEL W. SPRAGUE

EDITED BY PAM REED

Mall Publishing Co.

THE PRINTED WORD THE PLANTED SEED

HIGHLAND PARK, ILLINOIS

Stories from Katrinaland

God Responds to Disaster in New Orleans

MICHAEL W. SPRAGUE

"Opportunities abound to share the message of thelove of Christ. Good rumors about the church are circulating everywhere. Wouldn't it be great if people didn't think of Christians as angry people carrying placards of protest or as self-righteous finger-pointing people? What if they saw a new humanity that displayed the fruits of the Spirit? What if Christians displayed both truth and grace in a way that reflected the real Jesus who came to seek and to save those who are lost? This is what I long for and am seeing. Please pray for a great revival." – Pastor Michael Sprague

EDITED BY PAM REED

Printed in the United States of America

Published by:
Mall Publishing Company
641 Homewood Avenue
Highland Park, Illinois 60035
Toll Free: 1-877-203-2453
E-mail: info@mallpublishing.biz
Website: www.mallpublishing.biz

All Scripture quotations unless indicated are taken from the Holy Bible: New American Standard Version.

Scripture quotations marked NIV are taken from the New International Version Bible.

We are indebted to NavPress for permission to reprint its illustration "The Bridge to Life" as an appendix.

ISBN: 1-934165-04-2

For licensing / copyright information, for additional copies or for use in specialized settings contact:

Trinity Evangelical Free Church
19380 North 10th Street
Covington, Louisiana 70433-8877

To God's First Responders,
an army of love
5,000 strong and growing,
and to the One Who sends them.

Contents

Foreword

Any pastor worth his salt welcomes the call of God in his life, but few would welcome a hurricane as the messenger of that call. Michael Sprague's initial reaction to the destructive force of Katrina wasn't one of rejoicing, but he was ready to set aside his strategic plan for Trinity Evangelical Free Church and follow where God was leading.

By fully surrendering their own agenda, Pastor Sprague and his team have become servants in the hands of a loving God, transforming a comfortable suburban New Orleans church into what Michael calls a "Kingdom Mobilization Center." Christians from across the country and around the world have partnered with Trinity church to meet the most basic needs of people who have lost everything they had.

Pastor Sprague has recorded the highs and lows of his post-Katrina experience, journaling for his readers the daily experiences of God's grace that he and his neighbors have received. Opening his worship services to these stories, he has heard and then reported a stream of divine appointments and life-changing exchanges experienced by volunteers and those they have served.

In these pages you will see the fingerprints of God all over the disaster relief efforts that were organized with the assistance of the Evangelical Free Church of America's Compassion Ministry. You will see how an ordinary group of believers were transformed into an Acts 2 church, and discover how the lives of volunteers were touched and changed, in some cases even more than the lives of those they came to serve. Most of all, you will encounter the God who provides, equipping a suburban pastor to shepherd a constantly changing flock, and using His church to meet the needs of hurting people whose lives were devastated by the storm.

Now, a year into the clean-up, it's time to tell these stories. They will inspire you to seek God's call on your own life and to answer that call in ways you've never imagined. I commend this volume to you as a window on the extraordinary work that God has been doing in the wake of Katrina.

Colin S. Smith
Unlocking the Bible

Introduction

On August 29, 2005, a category five hurricane named Katrina came onshore along the Gulf Coast of the United States, measuring sustained wind speeds of 125 mph and wiping out entire coastal communities.

The City of New Orleans, built below sea level, had a levee system in place intended to withstand the pounding of such tropical storms but equipped to handle them only up to category three. Though Katrina had weakened to that lower rank, it wasn't long before the levees gave way to the force of the storm surge water brought in from the Gulf of Mexico, and one of America's biggest natural disasters was under way.

While roof-top rescues in New Orleans were receiving nationwide attention, filling the 24-hour news cycle, a 700-member Evangelical Free Church named Trinity on the north end of Lake Pontchartrain was quickly becoming a hub for relief efforts for the entire Northshore community. And Pastor Michael Sprague began a series of open letters on Trinity's website to communicate with the Trinity family and tell the stories of God's response to Katrina through the Trinity relief efforts.

During the next 11 months Pastor Sprague would see this "cozy suburban church" turned into what a team leader called "the church of the stained carpet," with a free store and a "campground" for some 5,000 volunteers right in Trinity's worship center. Over time, the Free Church of America's Compassion Ministries sent Mark Lewis and his family from Pennsylvania to come alongside Pastor Sprague to "run the teams."

Homes, businesses, and relationships have been rebuilt and transformed through the work of what Pastor Sprague has dubbed an "Army of Love." The work is continuous, the stories inspiring, and the change has been remarkable in the lives of those serving as well as those served. But then, it's God Who is truly in charge, and Pastor Sprague is fully aware of His authority.

Pam Reed

August 2006

AUGUST 31

Sunday I preached to a remnant of 25 people on the story of David and Goliath. The take home message was "The Battle is the Lord's." I am sure we will have to put that into practice over the coming months. After preaching, we decided we'd better flee the storm. We are currently in Birmingham, Alabama, desperately wanting to return to help people in our area. It is so hard to get information. We have been told that one in 20 trees are down in our neighborhood and the town of Slidell next to us lost 200,000 trees. Power, sewage, gas may be out for months. This condition is a 1,000-fold better than our friends and neighbors in New Orleans. The conditions are deteriorating and every indication is that it is a war zone — suffering, misery, and the human toll. We are with other refugees of the Gulf coast who share their concern for lost spouses, friends, and homes that are surely gone.

These surely are the days that God's grace abounds in the midst of chaos.

Please pray for revival on the Gulf coast. There is no one to depend upon but the Lord. Pray for the church to be at its absolute best over the next few months. This means abiding in Jesus and allowing for His supernatural resources to flow through us. Pray for strength and wisdom to respond as Jesus would want us to in the middle of this storm. It is staggering to think of resources that will be needed to rebuild homes, lives, hearts and souls in the coming days. By faith I believe Jesus will be sufficient.

Your friend,

Michael

SEPTEMBER 1

The reports of devastation continue to intensify. We talk to people with missing spouses, brothers, and children. People are confused, shell-shocked, and perplexed. It is so hard to get information. The reports suggest that life will not be the same for months, and the truth is probably that it will never be the same.

Donna and I plan on returning to Mandeville/Covington tomorrow to be part of the solution. We are told one in 20 trees are down in our area and that Slidell looks like it has been through a nuclear explosion. Much ministry awaits in physical and spiritual needs.

We are reminded in this that life does not consist in the things which we possess. Jesus is our life and sufficiency. We are "betting the farm on God." The Old Testament illustrates that God does some of His best among refugees, and He is always faithful. My prayer is that this season will see the church being at its best — serving, loving, caring, and pointing people to a Deliverer.

Betting the Farm on God,

Michael

SEPTEMBER 2

Well, we finally got the word about our home. All of our large pine trees came down either fully or snapped part way up. One went through the house and is occupying a second floor room. Apparently, someone nailed a tarp on the roof to keep out as much rain as possible. Whoever you are — Thank You! Like so many, we will be in the process of figuring this all out. Fortunately, the rest of the pines fell away from the house and didn't hit the neighbors. The fences are down, and it must look like a war zone.

Donna and I are attempting to head back in tomorrow. There is no power, water, sewage, telephone, etc. We will trust God for provision and may have to camp out! I understand electric lines are down throughout the church lot and one tree exploded the swing set equipment.

Please pray for:

1. The vast numbers of people who are missing loved ones. Some are surely gone, some misplaced, and some without communication. The stories are devastating.

2. That Trinity Church would be raised up to be all the Lord would want us to be in this crisis. Isn't that what we are called to do? People from across the country have e-mailed me today to express concern and offer help — resources, encouragement, manpower, etc. I can't tell you how much that helped. On Monday, I will meet with a leader from the E-Free Church. He represents over 1400 churches, and Trinity may be able to be used as a staging area for ministry on the Northshore and eventually into the city. My home church in Maryland has offered to help in any way possible. Individuals have volunteered to come to us. There is nothing like the local church when the local church is working right.

3. God to be glorified in the midst of great devastation. What would we do without Him!

In closing, thanks for your prayers. Something like this certainly simplifies life. Donna and I wondered for the last week what the empty nest syndrome would bring us. Now we know.

Still Betting the Farm on God,

Michael

SEPTEMBER 3

Donna and I are home today. It is not the same home or city we left, but it is home. People are starting to re-emerge, huge military planes are refueling helicopters high above our heads, the sun is shining, and best of all, God is on the throne.

There is nothing like a hurricane to turn your world and life upside down, but God provides. We came back trusting God for everything, and He is providing.

1. We needed a place to sleep, and God gave us a friend to bunk in with seven people in one room. That works!

2. Another friend provided his home for us to stay during the next three - four days with a generator. In case you don't know, a tree is sitting on our house, some water damage, etc.

3. God sent two seminary students from Chicago to help wherever they could. They are helping us dig out.

4. Someone is painting a sign for us that we will hold services outside tomorrow at 9. No power, and probably not for awhile.

Please pray for the overwhelming needs:

1. There is much work to do here, though New Orleans and Slidell are so much worse. It is hard to contemplate how life will go on for so many. The economic devastation is mind-boggling. Where will people work? How will people survive? Only God can provide! I expect to open two emergency funds to help with Hurricane Relief — Efforts for the needy and an emergency fund to keep the church afloat.

2. Pray for safety. Many are carrying guns. Neighborhood watches are established to keep looters out. Signs read, "Looters will be shot." Everyone is watching out for everyone else. The best and occasionally worst in people is showing itself.

3. Pray for revival in our land. Who is there to trust in but God? We believe life is hard, hell is hot, yet God is good. He alone is our sufficiency. Now is the time to trust God for salvation and daily provision. If you don't know the Lord, please trust Him today.

Communication is so difficult. I will try and communicate all that I can. In closing, I believe God's promises are true, and He will save us from this destruction. I look forward to recounting His faithfulness.

Michael

P.S. I'm now hooked up to a laptop and a generator. Individuals and churches are contacting me by e-mail to see how resources can be coordinated (money, manpower, supplies, etc.) What encouragement. Thank God.

SEPTEMBER 4

Dear Trinity Family,

The wind has blown, the waters have moved through, the sun is shining, the trees are down, military tanker planes are circling overhead refueling helicopters, work crews are beginning to move in, and best of all, God is on the throne. I believe God for ALL of His promises. One day, the stories of His faithfulness will be extraordinary.

I'm sure in many ways the pressure of these events weighs heavy. Our lives will never be the same, but God can bring beauty out of ashes. Donna and I returned to find a tree in the middle of our house, and a "nuclear explosion" of nine downed pines occupies the back yard. In time, God will provide everything we need. The church building is intact with a little water damage and a number of trees down on the property. Again, God will provide in His time.

How are you? We are poised to trust God and pull together as a church family. The web-page, www.trinitychurchonline.net, has a new section to collect reports on your location, needs, and experiences. Let us know. We need to check on each person. <u>Please</u> let us know. We care! You are loved! We want to know you are O.K.!

Many churches across the country want to help us and use Trinity as a staging ground for meeting needs in our community and region. We have been blessed in many ways, and God wants us to extend that to others. Pray for a mighty spiritual move of God's Spirit.

Finally, remember to trust God, take one day at a time, don't shrink back, let your light shine, and remember God will make a way because He is ABLE. Preach the gospel at all times, and if necessary, use words.

Betting the Farm on God,

Michael

SEPTEMBER 4

There is nothing like meeting for church with a remnant of 50 people who are simply glad to be alive. The simplicity of life and the gratefulness of people are breathtakingly good. The stories of God's goodness in the storm are inspiring.

A young Mexican man bicycled out of Slidell in the middle of the hurricane and survived. One of our people found him having not eaten since the storm, and took care of his needs.

Last night I had dinner with a man whose brother-in-law fled to Houston with his family. On the way they realized all their money was gone. Imagine no money, not knowing what's next for their family. Of course, this puts a little stress on marital communication, and in the midst of an argument, the man hit 75 in a 45 mph zone and saw flashing lights. The family pulled over. The wife looked out of the back window and saw her husband sobbing and the policeman patting him on the shoulder. Shortly afterwards, her husband walked up to the car carrying a wad of cash. The officer had emptied his wallet into this man's life. **Wow!** My guess is that they didn't report this on television.

As I write, two huge military helicopters landed a stone's throw from where I am standing. Thank God for the military, police, fire, electrical, FEMA, Red Cross, etc. who are starting to pour into our area. Some electricity was restored along the highway today.

Please pray:

1. Jo Swan found out her uncle drowned today. Two city officials committed suicide from the stress, many, many families are dispersed, paychecks are jeopardized, and everyone is trying to make it up as they go along. Pray for comfort, wisdom, peace, creativity, ingenuity, and everything else.

2. Pray for a 9:00 a.m. meeting with Jim from the EFCA tomorrow morning who can help us coordinate the efforts of 1400+ churches across the country. Trinity is in an extremely strategic location to be used as a staging ground over the year.

3. Pray for resources. Trinity Church has opened up two emergency accounts in response to the hurricane disaster.

Hurricane Survival Fund
This is a fund for Trinity Church to simply stay afloat financially. No offerings have been taken the last two weeks, and only a remnant remains here. People are scattered throughout the south, and it will be months before any semblance of normalcy returns.

Hurricane Relief Fund
This fund will be administered by Trinity Church to assist the displaced, poor, and needy with help with food, clothing, housing, money, etc. The needs are great, and we are called to serve this community. Our intent is to preach the gospel at all times, and if necessary, use words. Spiritual and material needs will be a priority.

If you don't designate a fund, we will trust God to lead us as to where to distribute the funds.

CHECKS CAN BE SENT TO TRINITY CHURCH, 19380 N. 10th STREET, COVINGTON, LA 70433

The outpouring of letters I am getting by e-mail is life-giving and encouraging. The expression of generosity is extraordinary. When I shared with with people this morning, there were tears of delight and smiles of hope. We are trusting God and partnering with you. Thank you.

Still Betting the Farm on God,

Michael

SEPTEMBER 5

What a good day. I met with Jim Snyder who is the head of Compassion Ministries for 1400+ churches with the Evangelical Free Church. Trinity Church will be used as a staging area for relief efforts throughout the Northshore and New Orleans region. Several staff with the Evangelical Free Church will join our staff over the next six to nine months to coordinate these efforts. Specific information is available on our website www.trinitychurchonline.net on how people from across the country can get involved giving, sending supplies and manpower.

Work is progressing. Most of the staff is back, and we are getting mobilized. One of the guys brought a team into a local town to clean up people's homes. The mayor was astounded at the generosity. He said, *"I used to think all Christians were hypocrites, but now I'm thinking otherwise."* That's what happens when work is done in the name of Jesus.

Please pray for:

1. Tracking down all of our displaced Trinity Church family. It is agonizing as a church shepherd, realizing the flock is scattered and unaccounted for. Of course, the good Shepherd knows the whereabouts of each one. If you are part of the Trinity family, please email or call us as to your location and needs. There is also a message board/ blog at http://trinitychurch.blogspot.com to report information.

2. Pray for 5,000 - 10,000 square footage of warehouse space and loading dock to collect truckloads of

supplies. Pray for 60 men who are working in the neighborhoods and sleeping on the church floor the next few nights.

3. Pray for perseverance, patience, and wisdom. We were counseled today to realize that this job will take months or years. As Americans we can get frustrated when we can't accomplish everything instantly.

4. Pray for revival in our land. Instead of trusting our strength or wits to get us out of this, we must trust God. This makes sense since He can split a Red Sea and raise the dead! He has always delivered the needy, and He will do it again as we humble ourselves before Him.

Michael

P.S. A possible answer to prayer. Since writing this letter, God may have provided a 20,000-square-foot warehouse. Pray for the 8 am meeting tomorrow morning. Praise for a compassionate, generous CEO.

Also pray for the 12 police officers who are coming in momentarily to help with relief efforts from Indiana.

SEPTEMBER 7 **What I Learned Today**

What I have learned today is, *"Ask, and it will be given to you; seek and you will find; knock, and it will be opened to you. For everyone who asks receives, and he who seeks finds, and to him who knocks it will be opened. Or what man is there among you who, when his son asks for a loaf, will give him a stone? Or if he asks for a fish, he will not give him a snake, will he? If you then, being evil, know how to give good gifts to your children, how much more will your Father Who is in heaven give what is good to those who ask Him*!"

Today I spent my life at two ground zeros. Half my day was spent at ground zero in New Orleans with 19 helicopters hovering above my head, scores of mobilized military units patrolling, 60% of the city under water. Dear people who rode out the storm [are] asking for nothing but ice, treasured well known sections of the city have become ghost towns, there are flipped cars, and buildings ... have been turned to rubbish. A hellish scene to be sure. My heart breaks for the residents of New Orleans, yet there is a remarkable determination by everyone to rebuild.

My personal ground zero centered around the command center of trying to pastor a local church in a devastated community on the Northshore of New Orleans. The needs are overwhelming and resources so seemingly inadequate. The situation is so impossible that we who are used to trusting in our own strength, wit, and resourcefulness were forced to trust God totally. What a novel idea to depend on the God who provides manna from heaven and the God who raises the dead.

Here is what I learned today

1. We decided we needed 5,000 to 10,000 square feet of warehouse space to accommodate truckloads of disaster supplies over the next six months. What does a pastor know about warehouse space? In fact, someone said, *"You'll never find it around here."* We decided to ask the Father specifically. By the end of the day, we had secured the space.

2. We needed a semi truck trailer on site immediately. What do I know about semis? I told my associate to get us one. He looked at me like I was crazy. I said, *"Go into town, and find someone with a semi, and tell him God needs a truck."* He found someone and asked, and he said, *"Well, okay, take it,and by the way, do you have a cab and truck driver to get it to the church property?"* His answer was, of course *"NO,"* but the man standing next to him had a cab and time to do it. **WOW** – what a novel idea to ask the Father.

3. We started to make this a habit during the day. It seemed like the Father wanted us in New Orleans. We

went to military checkpoint after military checkpoint without official credentials and only a credit card of a food relief worker. At six checkpoints, hardnosed military gatekeepers with machine guns mysteriously waved us through so we could assess needs and talk to the remnant who rode out Katrina. **It was the Father again.**

4. I had no firm place for my family and three sets of missionary guests to spend the night and plan for food for dinner. I told my wife to take care of it. *How*? Ask the Holy Spirit to supernaturally provide. *Oh? Oh, okay.* Within a few hours the call came that freed a house for one more night. What about dinner? Donna literally bumped into a woman who had just bought food to feed 12 emergency workers who were sleeping on her floor. Yet she was disappointed because they were called out on a security detail in Slidell from 6 pm to 6 am. What would she do with the food? Donna said to her friend, *"Michael said the Holy Spirit would provide us dinner for tonight, so I guess all that food was designed for us."* Our wonderful friend smiled and provided us the manna God sent from heaven.

5. I needed a generator, so I was now getting into this "asking the Father" approach rather than the figure-it-out-myself approach. Within hours I had one generator at my house and another at my office with an A/C window unit thrown in. **WOW**! But what does a mechanically challenged klutz like me know about installing generators? Call came in, *"Michael, my husband can stop by and get it set up."* **Wow again**!

6. We needed someone to clear the big pines that had fallen all over the church property covering sections of the parking lot so truckloads of supplies could come through. When I returned, 12 S.W.A.T. team members from Indiana had totally cleared the lot and stacked the

wood and debris. They thought their mission was to provide security in Gulfport, but FEMA kicked them out. Then, someone else didn't want them. I guess the Father wanted them at our place. We bunked them all in a house where the sign entering the neighborhood read *"Looters will be shot."* If looters tried to get into that house last night, WATCH OUT! You should have seen their arsenal of weaponry.

7. I still pondered throughout the day, *"How will Trinity Church survive financially?"* No offerings, people scattered, many jobs gone, some already not planning on returning, new building under construction, etc, etc. Right at midnight I opened an e-mail. I read it and cried. A young girl in Maryland overheard her mom and dad discussing our plight. She went to her room and brought back her entire piggy bank and said we could have all her money, and if they could remove her loose tooth, there would be enough money to buy one Barbie doll for a little refugee girl. Again the Father showed He would provide.

I could go on with more stories but you get the point, I trust. This pastor is learning a new approach to living. I've gone each day to my ground zero without touching any money or seeing one newspaper, and seeing very little news. Yet, I have had all I've needed. And every meal has been provided by the Father. **Yea, God!** At 10 something at night, someone came and asked me for two workers to do some tree work in Mississippi tomorrow. My first thought was, *"What do I know about tree workers in Mississippi?"* Yet, what I said was, *"I think we should ask the Father for two laborers to supernaturally show up tomorrow."*

Whatever your need is today, you might try asking the Father. What a novel idea!

Michael

P.S. This really did happen in one day.

A sign of the pain that has followed Katrina.

SEPTEMBER 9 **Time in New Orleans**

Yesterday afternoon I crossed through six military checkpoints in the process of assessing the needs and opportunities with our missionaries with Urban Impact Ministries. I accompanied two of the leaders, Scott and Melanie Lundeen. There were 19 military helicopters high above and a military-run city down below. This was not the city of jazz, streetcars, and beignets I once knew.

Our mission was to investigate Urban Impact's neighborhood and assess damage and opportunities for ministry. Their neighborhood was among the hardest hit. The church building was dry, but much of the neighborhood was under water. Imagine your home and all your things destroyed. We talked to people who decided to ride it out. It wasn't the storm that did the damage but the levee break and the water that poured in. The Convention Center has a stench so bad it was unbearable, we were told, and yet that's where the only food and water resided. The military came through every 20 minutes on patrol and urged mandatory evacuation. I can tell you those people of New Orleans weren't going anywhere unless they were dragged out. They were all worried that everything they had would be stolen if they left. They had pit bulls and guns to protect their minimal earthly belongings. A few blocks over we observed a military operation in process as the Indiana National Guard was searching for a man who had fired shots.

We then went over to Urban Impact's newly purchased property. What a scene! The Superdome was just above them, representing New Orleans. Below them was water, ruin, rubbish, turned over cars, and crashed vehicles — and a broken-down hearse. All this pictured death. I then looked at the new property that through the eyes of faith I could see as a beautiful new ministry-oriented building for Urban Impact. This represented life. In the midst of carnage, death, and destruction, I choose to believe in God for resurrection power and the promise to bring beauty out of ashes. There are tears now, but joy will come in the morning. What a day that will be. Pray for New Orleans and our missionaries at Urban Impact.

Michael

SEPTEMBER 10

My life is being taken through an amazing turn of events. I have worked for months on a major strategic planning initiative. After months of planning, meetings, tweaking, and messaging, finally a couple of weeks ago, it was unanimously approved by our leadership. A week ago God decided to blow up my plan with a hurricane named Katrina.

I think He laughed at my plan and said, *"I can do better."* I think He will get more accomplished by His plan. I believe He wants to accomplish great and mighty things through the road of messiness. I believe He finally has our attention — in fact, maybe even the nation's. I choose to join His plan. Even though I don't know the future, I know the One Who holds the future.

In the middle of this crisis, it is evident that everyone everywhere needs the Lord. When we fail to humble ourselves before Him or depend on His strength, He must laugh. He sure has my attention. How about you? If you don't know Christ, trust in the One Who died for your sins and rose from the dead. God loved you so much, He gave His only Son. If you believe in Him, you will be saved, secure, and full of peace with God. Stop and call on His name, and He will save you. Guaranteed!

If you made a strategic life plan like me and realize God has a different path for you, turn around. Get off the old path and on to the new. Take the "Father first" path. Voice the words, *"Not my will but Thine be done."* This path may be a little scary and wild, but it will be the ride of a lifetime. I'm finding that out. **Yea, God!**

Michael

SEPTEMBER 12

Here is a quick note to keep you in the loop and help you to pray specifically. Here is a sampling of the human toll, interacting with folks in the last day:

1. A church family lost their house completely in Slidell. Everything is gone. Yet a couple drove their 5th wheel from Michigan and gave it to them for free. God provided. **Yea, God!**

2. Another family lost their home. Trees destroyed it. Someone is letting them live in their home until December. **Yea, God!**

3. An attorney lost his entire law office. The hurricane set off the sprinkler system, and it rained inside the building for two days. The building needs to be gutted. **Pray.**

4. My staff helped a tough 80-year-old man remove debris. He started to cry and said this was the first time in his life anyone has ever helped him for nothing.

5. One family stopped into the church after seeing our sign *"Free Food, Free Water."* We helped them, and

then the team gathered around and prayed for a specific family need. One hour later they called and said God answered the prayer and their faith was restored.

6. One man I talked to had yet to hear if many of his New Orleans relatives survived Katrina, and he was searching desperately for them.

7. One Middle Eastern man wanted to know if Katrina was God's judgment on the French Quarter and New Orleans for wickedness. This question gave me an opportunity to share the gospel of Christ.

8. One of our men had a Mexican young man show up on his property. He was lonely, disoriented, and hungry. He had bicycled out of Slidell in the hurricane to escape the flood waters. He had not eaten for days and didn't know where to go.

The list could go on and on. Everyone has a story.

Praise:

1. Power is being restored to neighborhoods immediately surrounding the church.

2. Relief teams have arrived from California, Ohio, Maryland, and Illinois. A team from North Carolina comes tomorrow. A man came from Texas to cook for the teams.

3. We had a Spirit-led, God-honoring worship service yesterday. We rejoiced in being alive. The church is being the church — caring, loving, listening, mobilizing.

Prayer:

1. Pray for spiritual revival and renewal. God has our attention. Pray for a spirit of surrender and yieldedness to the calls of God.

2. Pray that we let our light shine in such a way that people see our good works and glorify our Father Who is in heaven. Thishappens one person at a time. As one person said, *"Jesus is in us. Now He wants to come out of us."* The opportunities are endless. Last night our half-dazed, hot, and tired neighbors were outside. With no A/C since the hurricane, they weren't sleeping at night. After getting a generator in our bedroom, we invited them to stay in our bed, and we went to another house. They were grateful.

3. Pray for my staff. Burnout is easy in these situations, and we have just set up a rotation to get people out for two days at a time.

4. Pray for wisdom in setting up organizational structures to sustain the effort over many months.

5. Pray for our church families who have no jobs or who have jobs now in jeopardy. Pray for those who lost homes or have great damage. Pray for wisdom, as schools are out and life is difficult. My guess is that over half the church is scattered throughout the south. Some people are moving out of state. Pray for wisdom.

There is so much more. Got to go. Ask the Holy Spirit to take my meager prayers and communicate them right to the Father. He will!

Betting the Farm on God,

Michael

SEPTEMBER 14 **New Update**

Let me start today by telling you how a hurricane can utterly transform the nature of a local church. Our vision at Trinity Church is to help people become fully devoted followers of Christ and then impact the Northshore, New Orleans, and beyond. We have determined to be intentional in getting outside of our walls and touching people's lives one by one with the love of Christ. I can tell you we have been kicked into high gear.

Trinity Church used to be a nice Christ-loving suburban church doing a good work. We are now a dangerous, outwardly focused, moment-by-moment, Spirit-dependent church doing Kingdom work. We now look like a Kingdom Mobilization Center.

1. Ministry Teams — The church is filled with ministry teams from all over the country. There have been more than 78 volunteers from at least eight states. The volunteers have performed an estimated 1,680 man-hours of work. We deploy the teams daily (8 am to 6 pm) to the most strategic needy areas of the community. This includes cutting seniors out of their homes for the first time; debris removal and chain saw work in homes; delivering food, water, etc., to hard-hit areas; medical relief into Mississippi; supplies to shelters, etc., etc. In the evening you find sleeping bags spread all over the facility.

2. Free store — On the major highway by the church, we have a sign that reads *"Trinity Church — Free Water, Free Food"* and the service times.

   There is a constant flow of people coming into the church for counsel and tangible help. The worship center has a free store where people can "shop" for groceries and personal needs.

3. Distribution System — We are running a warehouse, and truck shipments bring in all kinds of supplies. Teams sort the items, and work teams distribute the supplies to shelters and the community daily.

4. Childcare Center — The church has retooled to accommodate up to 100 children a day for free to

businesses in the area so their employees can work. The Red Cross brings in emergency meals to feed the children.

5. Food Preparation — We are cooking breakfast, lunch, and dinner for large numbers of people. Teams have to stay strong, and the fellowship is incredible. We provided a meal for the whole congregation Sunday. We will do that again tonight and Sunday.

6. Housing Volunteers — The property is filled as well. A tent encampment of workers occupies our ball fields, and an RV and cars fill the lots. We understand a portable shower unit is being worked on. We are bringing in two 5th wheels to provide housing and office space.

7. Shepherding — Phone calling teams are at work contacting every person at Trinity to assess their location, needs, and availability for ministry. We have connected with about half of the church body, but many are scattered throughout the south. Pray for this pastor who wants to know the condition of his flock.

8. Urban Impact — I have been interacting closely with Scott Lundeen. We are thinking through logistics on how Trinity Church can be a launching pad for supplies and work teams to rebuild and evangelize in the city of New Orleans. We are committed to a strategic partnership with Castle Rock and Urban Impact [inner city New Orleans ministries].

9. Counseling — The ministry of encouragement and comfort is being extended to people throughout the community. Yesterday, I talked to a dad who just couldn't stop crying. His needs were so overwhelming. I couldn't imagine being in his shoes, yet we both were trusting God would make a way. Along with words and prayer, we arranged for the man to have housing with

one of our members, food, clothing for his young son, and toys. Imagine being out on the street with nothing.

10. Services — Our normal attendance on Sundays used to be 700+. The last three weeks we have had 20, 50, and 300. We are now having one Sunday service at 10 am and a Wednesday service at 5 pm. The ministry of caring, prayer, sharing, loving has never been deeper. People who have never come to church are wandering into our building and services. Everyone has had their life turned upside down. Everyone has a story and an openness to talk. Our people are taking advantage of "divine appointments."

I have to go. There is so much to do. Pray for revival, strength, funds for Trinity Church, and wisdom to structure for sustained ministry and relief efforts. Pray for people — many are hurting. I don't think most of us realize or can anticipate how our lives have been changed. Pray for the church of Jesus Christ to have its finest hour of ministry for the glory of God.

Betting the Farm on God,

Michael

P.S. I just got a note from one of our displaced members. His words read, *"No electricity, but we have power! (in the Holy Spirit)."*

SEPTEMBER 16

I got a note from a friend yesterday who was hit hard from the hurricane. His wife was living in a different city, and he was here on the Northshore digging out. His words were written this way, *"No electricity, but we have power! (in the Holy Spirit)."* I trust you can say *"Amen"* from whatever the part of the country you reside, because the people of Trinity Church are experiencing this.

It's amazing how doors of opportunity are flying open as we serve people.

1. One woman I talked to had lost three children in the last few years and now lost her home. We helped her with supplies, and as I prayed that God would put her tears in a bottle as the scripture states, she wondered if God's bottle was big enough. She needed a church home and said she would come Sunday. Another man had his wife leave him this week, and he is homeless. Another woman lost everything.

2. Our free store has a constant flow of visitors. Each has a story of brokenness, hurt, and perplexity. Every encounter is a chance to share Christ, food, prayer, and love. **What a ministry!**

3. Last night, we served a free dinner and had a powerful sharing service. The testimonies of God's faithfulness in the midst of pain were Job-like. God's interventions are marvelous. Work team members have been transformed. People from the neighborhood stood and expressed astonishment that total strangers would clear their lots for free. The Holy Spirit was moving powerfully. Several people confessed that they may have caused the hurricane. They had beenpraying for the last year that revival would come to Trinity Church and New Orleans…. They'd prayed *"God, whatever it takes"*….After observing the last week, they were convinced the revival had begun.

4. Imagine another set of work teams going into Slidell with buckets, mops, and bleach willing to scrub out black mold that is everywhere. All kinds of people are asking, *"Who are you? Why are you doing this?"* Of course the answer is, Jesus Christ has changed their lives.

5. It's hard to describe the joy and exuberance of Trinity folks and team members from 13 states knit together in a purpose far bigger than we can describe. Though we

are weary in body, we are not weary in zeal and devotion. There is nothing more important to invest our lives in. The cause of Christ is worth it.

In closing, a thought about those who are saying this is God's judgment of New Orleans:

Someone told me this a few days ago, and I'm sure many are thinking this. Far be it from me to fully know the mind of God. He is both righteous and loving. Yet in Luke 13: 1 - 5, I find a similar train of thinking 2000 years ago. It seems Pilate killed a bunch of Galileans, and 18 people were killed when the tower of Siloam fell. As usual, religious folks assumed that this calamity was God's judgment upon the unrighteous. Jesus seems to think they had missed the point. Anyone can be killed. The worst thing in the world is not dying; it's dying without Christ, our Savior. Jesus is saying during devastating times, *"Do not point the finger of condemnation at others, but check your own heart."*

Do you have peace with God? He, of course, is the source of that peace.

My observation is that when people throw rocks at so-called sinners, those people get driven farther away. When people get loved and shown grace, they are drawn to the One Who saves from sin. I believe the people of New Orleans and the Northshore matter to God. I hope you do, too!

Betting the Farm on God,

Michael

P.S. Pray for our 10 am Sunday service and 11:30 am lunch together as a church family. Some of our people are just returning to town, and everyone needs the healing touch of the Lord. Pray for many displaced people and neighborhood people who will join us for the first time.

SEPTEMBER 17

Donna and I just returned from the town next to ours called Slidell. Maybe you have heard it mentioned on the news. We have numbers of people attend Trinity from Slidell. By phone I have interacted with a few who had their homes destroyed. The reports I was receiving were dire. However, it is one thing to hear about the devastation, and another thing to see it.

We observed community after community of total loss. Imagine home after home with everything in the home piled into the front yard eight feet high — beds, baby dolls, chairs, boats, and clothes — EVERYTHING in a junk heap. Imagine this continuing mile after mile after mile. Imagine communities with signs at the entrance that read, *"Come in and die!"*

Donna and I both were left with headaches and feeling sick to our stomachs, totally drained. Think of what these folks are feeling. I saw New Orleans early on with miles and miles of homes under water, and that impacted me. The impact of today's visual was far worse. I shudder to think what New Orleans will be like when hundreds of thousands of people return and will have to, likewise, pitch everything they own, creating mountains of loss and misery. I know our lives do not consist of the things we possess, but people are hurting. **Please pray.**

Now for the good news. Trinity has become a major mobilization center. Teams of workers have come in from about 15 states over the last two weeks and have been deployed to do the Father's work. It is amazing the vibrancy and zeal of these servants. They have come from Evangelical Free churches and a few others. Teams are deployed to deliver food, work with our free store, cut trees, mop black mold out of homes, deliver medical supplies, and consult with hospitals, shelters, local pastors, mayors, and community leaders. In the process of letting their light shine, people see the good works and glorify the Father in heaven. In the context of servanthood and love, everyone asks, *"Who are you? ... Why are you doing this?"* The answer is the *"Love of the Lord."*

A couple of stories may help you to see. For months, one man has been prayed for and has always resisted the Lord because of his involvement with the occult. He talks to ghosts. This man had a tremendous need at his home since 150 trees had fallen on his property. Our teams cut them up and helped him clean up. For the first time he allowed people to pray over him and was so emotionally moved, he couldn't talk the whole afternoon. A door is open, and it was a privilege to serve him.

Another 78-year-old man had to be rescued off his rooftop from the flood waters. After a few days he returned to his home, distraught and hardened. Our team helped him and showed love, and he bowed his head and trusted Christ as his Savior. **Yea, God!**

The church is being the church. Opportunities are endless. One by one, people are being met and helped in the name of the Lord. God is bringing beauty out of ashes. Praise His name.

Betting the Farm on God,

Michael

Where do you go for hope
when your whole world has collapsed?

SEPTEMBER 22

It is amazing how one event called Katrina can be used by God to transform a local church. As persecution in Acts 8: 1 scattered the early church, so a hurricane has shaken us to our core. Yet, God is good and is bringing beauty out of ashes.

If you walked into Trinity Church, you may not recognize it anymore. Our nice, safe, comfortable, structured, suburban church does not exist anymore. We are an unsafe, uncomfortable, dangerous, outwardly focused, moment-by-moment, Spirit-dependent church, asking Jesus *"What's next?"* We are weary yet count it a privilege to be part of the cause of Christ.

Just like in Acts 2, we are seeing God's miraculous interventions.

1. At our Sunday service there were a sea of new faces present. About 25 people raised their hands to signify they wanted to trust Christ as their Savior. **Yea, God!**

2. One of our church families lost everything. Trees fell on their house, and they had eight feet of flood waters fill their home. Everything is gone. It will probably be bulldozed. We encouraged them to bring their little trailer to the church property to live. Half our church property has been without power. It was amazing to see the electric company show up and fix the power after one call. Late in the day three utility company trucks were driving down the street as this homeless couple was driving up the street. They had electricity for their little camper. He provides in big and small ways.

3. I finished a meeting on how we would operationally continue our free store. We were discussing the supply process, and as soon as the meeting was over, a woman we helped with food the day before walked in with God's answer — a Christian group who will drop off supplies daily. **Yea, God.**

(Note: Pray for our free store. There is a steady flow of traffic all day long. As folks fill up a box, they tell their story. After three minutes they start to cry. Life is so overwhelming. Yesterday, I helped a woman who lost her home totally and her business. Her three- and five-year-old grandchildren are missing. She was at Trinity Sunday and has moved in with one of our families. She is making Trinity her home church. Pray for Michelle, but realize there are thousands of Michelles. I'm sure you are seeing images on your TVs. Imagine the stories that are behind the images. People are worn out, discouraged, and yet desire hope.)

4. Several separated couples have gotten back together, and several separated couples are helping each other put the pieces of their lives back together. Another man reported that his marriage had never been better.

5. At our Trinity services we allow time for sharing. It is amazing to hear the stories of strangers from the community who show up and report how Trinity has helped them. They give glory to God! Our volunteers and church members are reporting God is turning their lives upside down. What a teachable moment!

6. For a church that has been crippled financially, God's promise of supply is what we cling to. Several churches and individuals and the Evangelical Free Church of America have generously sent or wired us money to function. We are amazed at the generosity.

Prayer requests:

1. Continue to pray for spiritual revival. It seems everyone is open to talking about the Lord. People are trusting. God has our attention.

2. Pray that Trinity Church never goes back to living the old way. We yearn for days of greater sanity and normalcy, but we never want to drift into comfortable Christianity. Pray God builds us deep in devotion for Christ and one another.

3. Pray for my weary staff. We are starting a staff rotation to provide days off. We need to run a marathon and not just a 50-yard dash. Pray God's encouragement on my staff. If you can think of any little ways to encourage, please follow the Spirit's promptings.

4. Pray for our church finances. I'll get a letter out soon that explains our financial situation.

5. Pray for hurting people. One leader was asking, *"God, why do You hate me?"* Another feels depressed. I don't even think the tidal wave of emotion has hit anyone yet. I believe four to six weeks from now there will be more needs than ever. Currently, we are all dealing with survival issues. Soon people will confront many other realities of living and change. Praise God that He loves the brokenhearted and saves those who are crushed in spirit.

Betting the Farm on God,

Michael

SEPTEMBER 23 **Teachable Moments**

There is nothing like a hurricane to build a teachable heart and have your internal radar system constantly being on the alert for the promptings of the Spirit of God. I wouldn't wish this calamity on anyone, but likewise I wouldn't trade for anything what I've been learning and how my life has been profoundly changed.

Here's one of the things I have learned. In the providence of God, I had a bunch of missionaries and relief workers bunking up with me in a house without power early on in the hurricane aftermath. One of them was a man named Pete, who was the Food for the Hungry tsunami director for the nation of Indonesia. God put this guy in the house I commandeered for a week at the beginning of this crisis. Isn't that awesome? I learned from him to be proactive and to have a bias for action. I learned that *"There is a solution for everything."* There was one more thing I learned that was huge. Pete says that in Indonesia many average people in tsunami-hit areas have had their entire worldview changed about Americans and Christians. The American military, churches, and relief organizations have been so exemplary in their conduct, service, and love that the people have embraced them deeply. Radical Islamic leaders preach hate for these groups, but the good works preach the real story. The people hear the angry words from their religious leaders, but reality communicates another story. Islamic people are wondering why the Islamic nations and churches haven't helped like the Christian groups have. These efforts have opened up a door of opportunity that was not there prior to the tsunami. The U.S. government, military, churches, and relief groups have created a relationship that will serve their various missions well for potentially decades to come.

There are deep implications from Pete's words for our situation in New Orleans and maybe even for the church in America. For three weeks we have been sending teams into our community to serve people for free. We want nothing in return but simply to display the love of Christ. These efforts have included food distribution, free store, cutting trees, taking medical supplies to hospitals and Red Cross stations, helping clean up flood-damaged homes, taking care of employees' kids for banks and businesses during the day, feeding displaced people, letting people sleep at the church, etc., etc. Our goal has been to serve others.

The result, however, has far exceeded anything we could have imagined. After the initial shock people have with teams serving them for nothing, they stand amazed and perplexed. Where does anyone ever give for free? How much do people experience being "Graced?" They ask, *"Who are you? Why are you doing this? Who are you with?"* The answer of course is, *"Jesus Christ."* I can tell you "good" rumors are spreading through the community about Trinity Church.

People are coming to the church on their own initiative to thank me, the pastor for our people. One person said, *"This is the most amazing church I have ever seen."* A local mayor whom we have been serving said, *"I used to think all Christians were hypocrites, but now I'm thinking a different way."* Last Sunday, a sea of new faces was in our church service, was in our church service, and 25 people raised their hands to indicate they prayed to trust Christ after the gospel was shared. Our people are getting into conversations daily with people in the community and sharing the hope that is in them. The stories I could be telling are endless.

I think this is it! Jesus's words in Matthew 5: 16 work. This truth is working in Indonesia and in New Orleans, and it will work in your back yard: *"Let your light shine before men in such a way that they may see your good works, and glorify your Father Who is in heaven."* If you get a chance to put this verse into practice in your sphere of life, let me know what God does through it. Expect a miracle.

Betting the Farm on God,

Michael

SEPTEMBER 24 **Topic: Surrender**

Life has changed forever for the people of the New Orleans region. Life will go on, but it will never be the same. I believe that will be true of my life as well. I'm a different person than I was a month ago. The simplicity of life and yet the struggle of life is unmistakable. The brief attempts to explain things or to predict the future are mind-boggling. The "misery quotient" of so many around me is off the charts.

On top of this, I believe the tidal wave of pain is yet to come. "Reality" has not yet hit home but will when the temporary props are removed. Fortunately, the one constant in the entire crisis has been the faithfulness of God. The reality of this is unmistakably and breathtakingly good. Hour by hour we ride the wave of the Holy Spirit, and He is supernaturally providing. The one thing I sense that He desires from us is simple devotion and surrender.

In some ways surrender has been easy. Desperate people have no other option but to surrender. I've been desperate day after day. There is no way I could figure this one out. My new way of life has been to cry out hourly to the Father. I ask, He provides. (Matthew 7: 7 - 11.) Maybe I shouldn't be so surprised. Maybe this is how He always wanted me to live — as a most cherished son of the most High God Who is my Father. His desire again is no more, no less than simple devotion and surrender.

Yet, in some ways, surrender is hard. Throughout all the chaos, long days, and destruction, Donna and I have said almost daily, *"Our one consolation in all this mess, is that Jonathan is safe in Texas."*

Note: For those of you who are just getting to know us, Jonathan is our only child. A week and a half before the hurricane, we dropped our son off as a freshman at Baylor University. Some said Donna went from the empty nest to no nest (a tree hit our house) in three weeks' time. Yet, our daily encouragement to each other has been that *"Jonathan is safe in Texas."*

Wednesday night, Trinity Church met together for a meal and a service. The theme was faith and God's care, from Psalm 40. Just as the service was beginning, I got a call from Jonathan. He informed me that Baylor's classes were being cancelled and the school would shut down Friday because Hurricane Rita was headed to Texas. Electricity would be shut off, and the kids should get water to drink and flush commodes, etc. As soon as I heard him say this, I chuckled inside and knew that God was speaking. *"Our one consolation, that Jonathan was safe in Texas"* was a prop that had to go. This world is never totally safe, yet ultimate safety is residing in the peace of God that surpasses all comprehension. Safety is not found in Texas but in surrender to the Lord daily. So, during the Wednesday service, I surrendered "Jonathan in Texas" to Jesus.

You should know that, as this drama has been playing out, I had been working on preaching on Genesis 22 this Sunday. This is the passage where God tells Abraham to take *"your son, your only son whom you love, and sacrifice him as a burnt offering on Mt. Moriah."* Isn't it interesting how there are no accidents with God! He still speaks.

Abraham heard his name spoken and knew the voice of God. Yet, the words must have seemed so strange. They made no sense. This was Abraham's dream, the child of promise. He must have been perplexed, undone, and confused. Yet, he walked the three-day walk to Mt. Moriah. It was a dark road.

Maybe you are there, too. You have been on a dark road to Moriah for a while. Your life is perplexing and hard. You don't know the end of your story. Abraham chose to surrender. He expressed simple devotion and surrender. Do you need to do this like I did? Is there a specific area or person you need to turn over to Him?

The promise Abraham stood on was this, *"God will provide."* Check it out in Genesis 22: 8, 14. God will provide! This is what I'm holding on to, and I ask you to do this as well. As God is making a way for us, He will make a way for you, too. The thing He desires is simple devotion and surrender.

Betting the Farm on God,

Michael

P.S. As I write I understand the levee in New Orleans has broken again. Many people will relive their trauma again. Where I live is under a mandatory evacuation tonight.

SEPTEMBER 26 **The Church That Jesus Built**

I wish all of you could experience Trinity Church as it is now. Often it is like Grand Central Station. People are everywhere. Tents, RVs, trucks, trailers, and vehicles fill the property. Inside, children inhabit the educational wing nursery as we continue our new childcare ministry for the businesses and community. The free store has a continual flow of weary refugees from every background you can imagine. Teams from Evangelical Free churches and other churches are deployed 8 am to 6 pm daily, and they eat, sleep, and fellowship throughout the campus. Makeshift offices with phones and computers are popping up throughout the building as little ministry groups meet to plan and then to launch out in the name of Jesus. On top of this, 500 people came to church yesterday to honor God, Who is worthy of our praise and thanksgiving. This included dozens of brand new people, including new believers and seekers. The church of Jesus Christ is being built. I feel like the turtle sitting on the fence post. When you see this phenomenon, you know the turtle didn't get there on its own. When you see what God has done at Trinity, you know we didn't do it ourselves.

Yesterday, in the service, many newcomers stood and gave praise to God for the teams that have reached out to them.

1. Marlow had been praying prior to the hurricane that God would redirect her life. Indeed, she has met the One Who gives her life. This former New Orleans travel guide who lost everything has been so energized by the Spirit, she is like the woman in John 4 who is telling an entire town about Jesus and Trinity Church.

2. Michelle lost her home and business and still hasn't located her three- and five-year-old grandchildren. She had only the clothes on her back, but she met people in the free store. Scared to death, she stepped into the service on Sunday and loved it!

3. Libby arrived back home after the hurricane to find her home half demolished. This moment of agony was diminished when a ministry team arrived at that moment to pray, comfort, and clean up her yard. What a divine appointment and God moment. She has come to Trinity for two weeks. Yesterday, she told the church family her daughter in Knoxville is all alone dying of cancer. A woman in the church made a call to the Evangelical Free church in that city to make a visit.

4. The local hospital ran out of juice for patients. A few of us thought, *"Could it be that juice bottles would come on our next truck?"* What came on the truck? **JUICE BOTTLES**!

5. A lady and her 16-year-old son fled Hurricane Rita from St. Charles. The woman's husband had died the day before from brain cancer. As she left town, a woman said, *"If you can't find a place to stay, look for a church."* Of course, as she drove east, there were no hotels available in the region. She went all the way to Mobile, Alabama. On her way back, she happened to

get off at our exit. She saw the Trinity sign and remembered her friend's advice. Upon hearing the story, our people ran out to greet them and said they could eat, shower, sleep, and be cared for as long as they needed.

6. One man found himself half dazed and crying out, *"God, why do You hate me? Why do You hate me?"* At that moment a team appeared and cleaned up his fallen trees. He's been at the church almost every day since then helping others.

7. One team found themselves in Slidell on Saturday helping at one home but couldn't miss hearing the neighbors in a huge altercation. They were arriving for the first time to see their cherished home crushed by water damage. The sight was too much to bear, and they let out all their emotions and anger on each other. It was unsettling that none of their family had come forth to help. The team decided to shift their efforts to this couple. They cleaned up the entire mess. The couple's hearts softened and grew large, as the day ended with prayer, hugs, love, and thanksgiving. God loved that couple through a team from California.

I could go on, but I'll stop here. I'll close with this today.

I love the story of the night Michael Jordan scored 69 points in one game. It was a blow-out, and at the end of the game, the coach pulled M.J. out and put in a little known sub who scored two meaningless points in the closing seconds of play. A few weeks later a reporter asked the sub, *"What is the highlight of your professional career?"* He said, *"The night Michael Jordan and I scored 71 points together."* This is how I feel about what Jesus is building at Trinity Church. He is doing the work, and it is a privilege to partner with Him in His Kingdom.

Betting the Farm on God,

Michael

P.S. Pray for a member of our church named Leroy. His brother was killed in the flooding, but the body washed away. They have taken DNA samples from the family to try to identify the body among the many unidentified bodies. This family shared at church yesterday how agonizing it is to not know.

SEPTEMBER 28 **An Army of Love**

Love is *"the final apologetic."* — Francis Schaeffer

"90% of evangelism is love." — Seminary Professor

"A new commandment I give to you, that you love one another, even as I have loved you, that you also love one another. By this all men will know that you are My disciples, if you have love for one another."

— Jesus (John 13: 34 - 35)

"Preach the gospel at all times, if necessary use words."

— A Drink at Joel's Place, Word Books, pp. 24, 36

"Let your light shine before men in such a way that they may see your good works and glorify your Father Who is in heaven."

— Jesus (Matthew 5: 16)

"...created in Christ Jesus to do good works, which God prepared in advance for us to do."

— Paul (Ephesians 2: 10 NIV)

"Live such good lives among the pagans that, though they accuse you of doing wrong, they may see your good deeds and glorify God."

— Peter (1 Peter 2: 12 NIV)

"The best argument for Christianity is Christians; their joy, their certainty, their completeness. But the strongest argument against Christianity is also Christians — when they are somber and joyless, when they are self-righteous and smug in complacent consecration, when they are narrow and repressive, then Christianity dies a thousand deaths."

— Sheldon Vanauken

A friend of mine asked me this morning about the challenges of maintaining a quiet time with God in the midst of the catastrophic crisis. I could certainly identify with having my neat, orderly routines turned upside down. However, upon reflection, I have concluded that I've never had such a vibrant time in meditating on some of the gems of truth God has burned into me over the years. The passages and quotes I started with have been at the forefront of my reflections and, more importantly, my observations of the workings of the Spirit.

Before my very eyes I'm seeing daily the gospel going forth courageously upon the shoulders of an army of bridge builders and love extenders. What evangelistic packages, intellectual arguments, political know-how, cultural relevancy, professional presentation, and every now and then a half-good sermon couldn't produce — love has produced. Love has proven to be the indispensable element.

At Trinity Evangelical Free Church, teams are going out daily, two-by-two or five-by-five. Armed with truckloads of mops, the "bleach brigade" descends upon a home. Armed with a shoulder to cry upon, women in the free store remain available. Armed with chain saws and bobcats, work crews clear the way. Armed with crayons and animal cookies, nursery and childcare workers free up moms and dads to work. Armed with medical supplies and juice, our doctor assists hospital staffs. Armed with truckloads of supplies, our drivers restock orphanages, shelters, and churches.

Day by day people ask, *"Why are you doing this? Who are you? Whom do you represent?"*

The answer is ***Jesus***.

This revolutionary approach involves "demonstration" preceding "proclamation." It involves deeds being wedded to words which make the witness more easily received. This army is made possible by a group of people who are fighting to carry a towel rather than desiring a throne. The vision is simply, *"Die to self"* and allow the Spirit to guide the rest. This daily surrender has created a love that bubbles to the surface, overflows, and eventually spills onto others.

By the end of this week our volunteer teams from around the nation will surpass 100. By the end of next week, the total will surpass 170. In addition to this, more and more church families are in a position to be deployed as well.

1. Please pray for the next two-week period of significant ministry.

2. Pray for leaders to manage logistics such as communication, work orders, feeding, sleeping, and equipment.

3. Pray for a bridge of love to be built and for boldness to share the hope that is within us.

4. Pray for a church like Acts 2 where "good rumors" were circulating in the community, where there wasn't a needy person among them, and people were coming to know the Lord daily.

5. Pray that the church really would be the church working right, and the residents of our community would say, *"I've got to check this out! This is what I've been looking for all my life! I've never seen anything like this before!"*

I can definitely see glimpses of this happening. It is a great day to be alive!

Betting the Farm on God,

Michael

SEPTEMBER 29 **Prayer**

What strikes me once again today is what an incredible "God Thing" is happening at Trinity Church. We did not make this up! We are not the one doing the internal "heart transformation" work. He is! We are amazed and thankful.

Here's a sampling from today:

1. In the hallway today a Trinity family returned to church after being a refugee family for weeks. Trinity is cluttered with people everywhere. The son said, *"This isn't our small cozy church!"* The mom said, *"No, isn't it beautiful!"*

2. Seekers are showing up at our free store and are helped. This week some came back. They started offering, *"What can I do? I just want to do something to help. I'll mop floors, anything. I am so grateful to you for your help. Please put me to work."* Another said, *"I'm just at home during the day. What can I do to help?"* (Her husband is away from home days at a time due to his work.) Yet another said, *"We can help while we are here. Put us to work!"*

3. Another woman who came back to the free store was also introduced to the "bridge illustration."* She affirmed faith in Christ, wants to be part of the church, have her child dedicated, and get married. **Pray.**

4. In the services this past week, a family walked in who had never been in a church before. They asked, *"What do we do?"* They had no idea. We helped them on their first day with God's people. **Pray.**

5. At the service last night, the sharing time was electrifying for me The first man to share stated he was from a different religious background but people from Trinity had helped him, encouraged him, and prayed for him. He was trying to understand what God was all about and doing in his life. **Pray as we follow up.**

6. Another lady from Ireland was here last week just after her husband died. She and her son had nowhere to go and nowhere to sleep. She saw the sign for Trinity and

has now moved in with a family at Trinity. They are amazed by the love of God's people, and they are hearing about our beautiful Savior.

7. Another man last night shared how his home flooded, and a Christian got him a 32-foot trailer to live in. **He praised God.**

8. People are e-mailing us and telling us God is changing their lives by hearing the stories of God. Others come and work and go back and tell the story. Only God could do this.

I could go on and on ...

I would like to ask you to pray for us. Remember in Exodus 17: 8 - 16, Israel was attacked by the Amalekites. Moses's strategy was to deploy Joshua to lead the troops, and Moses would pray. Moses went up on the hill and prayed. He raised his hands, signifying dependence on God. When Moses's hands were raised, Israel prevailed in battle. When his arms got weary and he put them down, the enemy made gains. All this happened before his eyes. Prayer turned the tide, and Israel prevailed in the end.

The point, I think, is that God's power comes through prayer. Prayer is not the preparation to the battle, but it is the battle. The prevailing power of God flows not through our wisdom, strength, or riches but through people who pray (Zechariah 4: 6). In fact, in Moses's situation he had two prayer partners to hold his arms up — Aaron and Hur. We need Aarons and Hurs! ... Would you do that for us?

Please pray for:

1. A great outpouring of the Spirit of God upon our region. Pray for revival and a new New Orleans.

2. Pray for the gospel to be spread more powerfully than ever and for thousands to walk through the doors of faith.

3. Pray for breakthroughs in marriages, wayward children, and with addictions.

4. Pray for finances and organizational wisdom. Teams are coming, and 200 people will be here next week. This will tax us to the limit. Pray for the support systems to deploy these good, zealous, wonderful servants.

5. Pray for Wayne Rogers, my worship pastor, who is producing a video to capture what God is doing and what the opportunity is.

6. Pray for stamina, strength, and wisdom for my staff. They arecourageous heroes whom God will reward in His due time.

7. Pray for the people of Trinity Church. Every person's life has been impacted. Things will never be the same. Imagine the hundreds of different responses and emotions that people are wrestling with.

   Pray for people's jobs, families, and finances. Pray for kids as school finally starts in our community on Monday.

8. Pray that we honor Christ. This is a time where great honor can go to Jesus or great dishonor. **Pray that this will be the church's finest hour.**

Betting the Farm on God,

Michael

***Bridge to Life,** © 1969 by The Navigators
See Appendix.

OCTOBER 3

A friend of mine wrote the following words to me:

"Gather in all that has happened since August — would the mighty wind of the Holy Spirit be seen like it is right now without the disaster? Would you have witnessed the mighty unstoppable Hand of God like you have without the hurricanes? Would Trinity Church have become 'Jesus with skin on' without a community desperately in need of His arms, His strength, His love? A community that suddenly had nothing but Him?"

"Nothing but Him" …. What a great statement and an apt description of who we are. Prior to Katrina, I had been meditating on an old C. S. Lewis statement, *"The man who has God and everything has no more than the man who has God and nothing."* Could C. S. Lewis be right?

I can tell you that many of the props to my life have been kicked out from under me over the past month — tap water, home to live in, electricity, newspapers, phones, computers, friends scattered — yet in a mystical sort of way I feel more alive, fruitful, and focused than ever before. Jesus really is the One Who gives life and life abundant.

The service yesterday at Trinity was so inspiring. God is showing up in ways that leave us inspired and encouraged.

1. "Spiderman" showed up at Trinity. Let me explain. Just before the hurricane, major newspapers carried the story of a local tree trimmer, nicknamed Spiderman, who had amazing agility over the years working at great heights in tall trees. He fell 65 feet from a tree and barely survived. Unknown to me, Spiderman's wife wandered into our free store last week for groceries and got an invitation to Trinity. During our sharing time, "Spiderman" from a wheelchair introduced himself and told his story. He has more broken bones in his body right now than Evel Knievel had in a lifetime. He gave glory to God for being alive and said he has found a new church home for his family at Trinity.

2. A team of 21 students from the University of Georgia went out on a work team Saturday. They met a woman in Slidell who had lost everything. Her house was flooded, three trees destroyed the frame, and she had been displaced. While living at a shelter, she was robbed several times. They helped her gather some belongings from her ravaged house and brought her to Trinity. At the first service her story was shared. One of our families made provision for her to live at a home in Slidell. Others met with her during our second service to pray and care. At the end of the second service, the word came to the auditorium that she had just prayed to receive Christ as her personal Savior. **We rejoiced!**

I could tell story after story — they never seem to end. God is so good to us. As has been said, *"You never know Jesus is all you need until Jesus is all you got, and then you know Jesus is all you need."*

Betting the Farm on God,

Michael

P.S. During the service we showed a 10-minute video production that highlights visually God's work over the past month and the devastation from Katrina. Pray that this would be used all over the country to glorify God and express the need. If you would like a copy, let us know. We haven't worked out yet how to cover costs, but we will soon.

OCTOBER 8 **New Mercies**

Tonight I just finished addressing a large group of our volunteers. We almost hit the 200 level! These are the best people you could ever meet. Let me tell you about a few:

1. One man came to serve even though his stepson died last week in a car accident. His stepson had wanted to come with his stepfather to serve in New Orleans.

Though grieving, he and his wife decided God had called them here. The stepfather brought his stepson's boots and laid them before the cross located at the front of the church. It is amazing how this family is sacrificing for us and our community. This man, a career military man, said he stood in shock and awe when he saw New Orleans. It is worse than anything he has ever seen in battle. He is making a difference.

2. Another man stood and shared that he was from Pacific Garden Mission in Chicago. Through his tears he shared that he had learned at the inner city mission to trust the Lord daily for food and life sustenance. He could see that we were doing the same, and tears came for the overwhelming need here. Here was a man with so little, giving so much to us.

3. One group from Illinois cancelled their "men's advance" (retreat) this month and brought their men here to serve us instead. They forfeited money through the cancellation but felt this was a great opportunity for their men to give of themselves.

4. Church after church verbalized that they were committed to us for the long haul. This is so encouraging, for the needs are so great. My observation is that life is getting harder for people, not easier. Power is coming back on, schools opened Monday, and FEMA is clearing the debris, but I am seeing the magnitude of the problems growing wider and deeper by the day. The props that got us through the first month are going away (Red Cross, National Guard, delayed mortgage and credit card payments, etc.).

Very soon we will face the realities of life, and in many cases it will not be pretty. Job lay-offs are reported every day, and this will have a spiral effect. Bills will come due soon, and many will collapse under their weight.

Many homes have two to five families living in them. Imagine the pressures living with several other families who have lost everything. I predict a tidal wave of human devastation in the next four to eight weeks as pressures mount.

I met with a family yesterday who lost their 14-year-old in the hurricane. They had two trees crash through their home, yet three families were now living in it. $60,000 worth of tools were stolen, and the man's employees were gone. The tears that flowed could have formed a puddle by the time we finished praying and helping them out financially. It will take years to put the community back together and see lives rebuilt.

In the middle of all this chaos, people are being helped one by one. That is the way of Christ. Hundreds of people have come into the free store. They are helped both spiritually and physically. Some of those helped in the free store now also work in the store and have begun attending church. Some have come to Christ within the last three weeks and have given testimony in our services. At least 52 new families have signed our visitor book at the church over the last few weeks.

Opportunities abound to share the message of the love of Christ. Good rumors about the church are circulating everywhere. Wouldn't it be great if people didn't think of Christians as angry people carrying placards of protest or as self-righteous finger-pointing people? What if they saw a new humanity that displayed the fruits of the Spirit? What if Christians displayed both truth and grace in a way that reflected the real Jesus Who came to seek and to save those who are lost? This is what I long for and am seeing. Please pray for a great revival.

Last Sunday I encouraged Trinity Church in three ways: **First, prayer: No revival has ever taken place without surrender and dependence upon God. Second, consecration: No revival in scripture or church history has occurred without repentance and coming clean with God. Third is love: We need to practically practice a supernatural kind of love so that there is not a needy person among us.** Pray for revival and renewal in our lives.

On a personal note, Donna and I had our roof rebuilt this week. The skylight from where the tree hit the house was huge. One day soon, three rooms in the house will need to be rebuilt, along with new carpet, and a new kitchen countertop. A new fence is being built tomorrow, and FEMA just removed the debris from our 10 trees.

Pray for Donna. As someone observed, Donna went from the empty nest to no nest in a week's time. She is back in her nest, but it has been messed with greatly. Donna continues to be a choice servant of Christ. Daily she ministers to others and enables me to focus on ministry. Her love for Christ and for me is outstanding. I am very grateful. We are bringing Jonathan back from Texas for a three-day weekend in two weeks so that he can get a firsthand look at our house and his room!

Well, the clock just struck midnight, so I'd better wrap this up. The Lord is good. I've got a great staff and a loving church. My wife is the best, and we cherish our son. I've got the best friends in the world who are all over this country. I've got a purpose to live for, enough problems to keep me dependent on God, and enough joys to keep me going. As I go to bed tonight, I realize that there is nothing I'd rather do than follow Christ.

Betting the Farm on God,

Michael

OCTOBER 10 **Stories**

I have marveled for a long time at how the book of John ends:

"And there are also many other things which Jesus did, which if they were written in detail, I suppose that even the world itself would not contain the books that would be written." —John 21:25

Wow! What are those stories? What a Life well lived. There is no one like Jesus, and I'm finding He is still creating story after story in the lives of people. In the service yesterday at Trinity Church, you couldn't help but sit on the edge of your seat wondering what God would do next.

1. The first man, a church member, shared how he had so many trees fall on his property, it took two-and-a-half

18-wheelers to haul away all of the debris. The company he hired was from Texas, and over the three days that they worked, he shared with the owner Jesus and God's way of living. At the end [the owner] bowed his head and prayed to receive Christ. When it was time to pay the man, he declared, *"You have hauled away more debris from my life than I have from your yard. You owe me nothing."* **Yea, God!**

2. A woman told her work team that, when they go back to Chicago, they were to tell their friends that *"You saved a life and a marriage."* This person told the story of how a work team had labored over days to dig out her family from the devastation.

3. A woman boasted of the love of God which was being shown through the people of Trinity. She told a story of one divine appointment after the next. I felt like I wanted to come out of my seat and cheer.

4. One team helped a man who was a Jehovah's Witness. He declared his affiliation, and one team member asked, *"But are you saved?"* He admitted he wasn't. They took the time to share the gospel, and God opened his eyes. He was saved by the power and blood of Jesus. **Yea, God!**

5. Remember Spiderman? The tree trimmer who fell 65 feet out of a tree and lived? He has more broken bones than Evel Knievel and is in great pain. His family and extended family were at Trinity on Sunday. They declared that they want to be baptized and join the church.

6. Another church member told about leading a person to Christ last Sunday during the second service. He started with these words, *"You came in here thinking you have lost everything, but you are about to gain*

everything." She did, because she met the Pearl of great price — Jesus!

7. Seth was the first volunteer we had at Trinity. Just after the hurricane hit, when things were really bad in Covington, Seth and his buddy Ryan left Trinity Seminary [Deerfield, Illinois] and headed south. They arrived when there was no electricity, and the city looked like it was hit by a nuclear explosion. They pioneered the work, and now hundreds of people have followed in their steps. Seth was back this week with a work team from Chicago … all valiant workers for Christ. Seth had to leave Sunday but told his parents, *"All I want for Christmas is a plane ticket to Trinity Church."* His heart is to come back and help us again. I told that story in the service, and a member of Trinity Church said, *"I will buy his plane ticket."* Seth, if you are reading this letter — **God provided!**

I preached yesterday on Revelation 2: 1 - 7 and commended my staff, Trinity Church, and the teams on their toil, labor, and perseverance. They are an awesome group of people who deserve a great *"Well done."*

The caution in the passage was to make sure we don't lose our first love. Ministry that flows out of devotion to Jesus is potent, but if we drift in intimacy with God and simply go through the motions, we become like travel agents passing out brochures to places we've never visited. To put it another way, the church that doesn't passionately love Jesus is like decaf coffee: Smells like coffee … tastes like coffee … looks like coffee … but has no punch.

Pray that Trinity Church remains a place head-over-heels in love with Jesus Christ and serves out of that strength. I can tell you that, at age 48, I'm finding Jesus more compelling, more interesting, more awesome, more surprising, more fulfilling, more attractive than ever. I pray that will be true of you as well.

Betting the Farm on God,

Michael

OCTOBER 13

This morning 15 staff (Trinity and Katrina) joined together for a couple of hours to plan for ministry that is sustainable over the next year or two. The structures we have now cannot accommodate the size of the project, so we are seeking God on how to super-size everything (offices, phones, communication, transportation, equipment, staff, computers, etc.) **Pray!** We all need to pull together for the next few weeks to make this work, and after that, we hope to have additional staff, equipment, and structures to get past "organized chaos" to "organized for the long run." With all the struggles, we are daily amazed what God is accomplishing through our inadequacies.

We started our staff meeting by focusing on celebrating the good work of God. If we go too fast, we will miss modern day burning bushes and the fingerprints of God. We are choosing to identify the sacred places and His divine imprints. If we choose only to live at a frantic speed, we will miss out on awe, wonder, celebration, and the peace that transcends our circumstances. I believe part of the revolution of our souls is to move us out of being superficial consumers to a people who celebrate.

In our case, the question is not if God is present; it's simply a matter of our awareness of Him. We choose to see the divine in the ordinary and sometimes glimpse the extraordinary. Our sharing and prayer time was filled with boasting in the new mercies of God.

Last night, during our sharing service, God showed up again.

1. One work team had cleaned up a home and got to lead a woman to faith in Christ. She was introduced at the services as a new believer. **What joy! We all celebrated.**

2. Another businessman revealed how God has revolutionalized his life. He has been helping a person who lost everything. He humbly admitted that a few months ago he would not have given a person like this a second's thought. Now he looks at people through the Father's eyes.

3. I read a letter from a modern day "woman with two mites." The letter read, *"I heard you on 'Open Line' tonight* [on Moody Broadcasting Network], *and enclosed is a $5 shopping card also good for gasoline use. I wish it could be more, but I'm only netting $130 per week (approx.) with no hope for advancement or wage increase. I'm sure I have much more than those in your area. I have some bread machines, pots and pans, a slow cooker, etc., I'd like to send to you when I have postage, if you want them .... I'm also a pet groomer, and if I was down there, I could help .... When I can add money to it (the card), I will. I will do the best that I can to add or send another card."*

   I am blown away by the generosity of this dear saint. She lives on $130 a week, yet is sending what she can to us. Please pray for God's abundance to be lavished on her.

4. Another woman shared how God has emboldened her to be open and authentic with the baggage in her life. She shared powerfully how God is at work and how living in truth and not in lies is freeing.

5. Another couple in our church boasted in God's provision of a free 5th wheel to live in. Their home was destroyed, yet God provided.

6. One team member was amazed and undone by God's ability to provide. He had come to Louisiana without the cord to recharge his cell phone and couldn't locate the right cell phone store in the area to get a new one. After his team completed a major tree clearing job, the team went deep into some bushes/tree area, and, oddly, there was a cord hanging from a bush. As they took a closer look, they were dumbfounded that it was the exact cell phone recharger that this man needed.

Coincidence or divine appointment? Had it gone through the hurricane? How did it appear in the middle of nowhere? **The fingerprints of God? I say *"yes!"***

7. Our office staff needed an additional staff person immediately, and prayers went up to God. Unbeknownst to them, a volunteer broke his foot in several places, and at the moment, all he can do is "office work." He called his employer back home, and the boss said that he had full disability coverage and he could stay here six weeks and work in our office. **God provides.**

I trust you, too, are looking for the fingerprints of God. As you see His fingerprints, boast in God Almighty. If you get a chance, let me know your story. I'm convinced God is all powerful and is strongly working among His people. Be strong and courageous. Be looking for His miracles.

Please pray for us:

1. Pray for the expansion of our ministry structures. We have a 14-inch skillet right now, and we need to get a 36-inch skillet to handle our enlarged "fishing" business.

2. Pray for a new children's pastor for Trinity Church. My wonderful part-time children's director Suzanne Cole informed me today that she will need to transition off the staff by the end of November. Suzanne will stay fully engaged in ministry at Trinity but recognizes that a full-time pastor is needed for the next season of ministry.

   She built the ministry upon the foundation of Jesus and made Sunday the best part of the week for many kids. Pray for Suzanne and for Trinity as we look to God's direction.

3. Pray for provision for our new children's ministry building. This building is going up right before our eyes and is desperately needed for ministry. The completion date is early next year. The building will be

used for our children's ministry, but God may have known we would also need to use this to house our Katrina staff and volunteer sleeping quarters. Our pledge system has collapsed since the hurricane hit, and we will need to pay the bank about $750,000 over the next few months. This amount seems huge to me, but I am trusting God for His direction. I'm convinced we were led to build this building, so we are pushing full-speed to finish it. **Pray hard!**

4. Pray for revival. This means renewal in hearts and repentance where needed. Luke 13: 4 - 5 in part addresses the question of how to respond to natural disasters like tsunamis, tornadoes, or Katrinas. The passage says, *"Or do you suppose that those 18 on whom the tower in Siloam fell and killed them were worse culprits than all the men who live in Jerusalem? I tell you, no, but unless you repent, you will all likewise perish."*

Jesus's response to this disaster may seem shocking. The amazing thing is not that a tower fell on 18 sinners, but that it didn't fall on all of us. We tend to put God on trial when calamity hits rather than putting ourselves on trial. God is calling the world to humility, surrender, and repentance. The truth is ... God is holy, and it is a miracle that I am breathing. I deserve separation from Him because of my sin, yet the good news is that Jesus did something for me that I never could have done for myself. Because of His substitutionary work on the cross, I can stand forgiven and reconciled to God. This is called **GRACE** ... God's free gift that is extended to an undeserving person. The gift of peace with God and forgiveness is offered as a free gift to any who are willing to humble themselves and trust Christ. The words of one man in scripture were, *"Be merciful to me, a sinner."* If you have never prayed to receive this gift of grace, sincerely pray this prayer to God:

"Lord Jesus Christ, I know I am a sinner and do not deserve eternal life. But, I believe You died and rose from the grave to purchase a place in heaven for me. Lord Jesus, come into my life; take control of my life; forgive my sins and save me. I repent of my sins and now place my trust in You for my salvation. I accept the free gift of eternal life."

If you prayed that prayer, let me know. It will absolutely make my day.

Betting the Farm on God,

Michael

OCTOBER 19 **The Church of the Stained Carpet**

A perplexing phenomenon is happening over and over with our work teams at Trinity that has me absolutely dumbfounded, not knowing quite what to think. As the groups leave, many profusely thank me for the opportunity they have had to serve and for the impact Trinity has had in blessing their lives. This seems so backwards. After all, we are the ones limping, crushed, hurting, desperate, and the recipients of the help. It seems to me that we should be thanking the teams one hundredfold for all that they are sacrificing for us. Yet, despite my best attempts at expressing gratitude and appreciation, groups thank me. Here is the pattern that emerged this week:

1. One woman, a church staff member of one of these churches, said, *"The people of Trinity are my heroes."* She explained that most churches, including hers, wouldn't turn their buildings into a Kingdom Mobilization Center with a free store in the worship center and people sleeping all over the building.

2. Another leader nicknamed Trinity, *"The church of the stained carpet."* He found delight that the church was manifesting an Acts 2 ministry and wished he didn't have to leave.

Pray for us.

3. Another group leader exclaimed for the first time in his life that he was seeing a church *"all used up."* He thought that is the way church ought to be done.

At Trinity, we are finding a new "normal" for doing church. Our building is not tidy, sanitized, or formal anymore; in fact, at times it may appear trashed from so much use. There is a constant buzz, and decisions flow out of kingdom availability as opposed to creating a "church look." The building is in constant use from the constant flow of people into the free store, work teams, and the reengagement of our church ministries. Our calling is to "die daily." As we surrender to Jesus, He energizes the ministry and makes a way. It may not all be pretty, but it is beautiful to behold. Lives are being transformed, and that makes everything worthwhile. This is harvest time, and so we choose not to shine up the tractor, plant the flowers in the garden, or paint the barn now. There may be a time for that later, we hope, but for now we choose to bring in the harvest.

Sharing time during the Sunday service was as electrifying as in past weeks. The stories of God's new mercies are exceedingly good, and we choose to recount these "burning bush" experiences publicly.

1. One man named Gene, from Wyoming, told of his team's experience this week helping a senior woman by clearing a long driveway that had so many trees down upon it, you couldn't even tell where the road was. With great labor, a bobcat, and chain saws, they labored over two days clearing a path. The woman was clearly overwhelmed but encouraged that someone would come to her rescue. The last day she had a doctor's appointment, and upon her return they asked her to experience the pleasure of once again driving down the driveway to her home. What she didn't know was that, while she was at her appointment, the team lined her driveway with balloons, and her porch contained a big sign that read, *"Love, Trinity Evangelical Free Church."* Tears of sorrow the day before turned into tears of joy. **Isn't the Kingdom of Jesus worth celebrating? There is nothing like it!**

2. We had college groups of 110, 36, 30, and 101 in this week from Trinity Seminary, Moody Bible Institute, Washington Bible College/Capital Bible Seminary, and University of Tennessee. These were among the finest young adults you could find anywhere. They were hardworking, Christ-honoring, and servant-hearted. Their enthusiasm was contagious, and we would delight in having them return. Many testified to God's work in their lives. One group got diverted from their work assignment because someone landed on a bee's nest. Yet, the hospital became their divine appointment. In the waiting room they got to share Christ with several in the hospital. Nothing can stop the work of Christ, not even a hornet's nest. **Yea, God!**

3. I read the letter in our service from a woman from Michigan who sent us a $5 gift certificate though she makes only $130 a week with no hope for career advancement. She wanted to help the people in Louisiana who have far less than she has. This modern day "woman with two mites" blew us all away with her extreme generosity and desire to send more when she can save another $5. After the service, someone left me with an envelope to send to this dear saint of Christ. It contained $100. You cannot out-give God. He is moving among His people so that people are seeing the "manna" of God. I thank God that He is redeeming people's lives and pocketbooks. **Yea, God!**

I preached from Revelation 3 on the church at Philadelphia. This was the church of the "open door." We are that church as God has opened a door for us. This is the opportunity of a lifetime. The fish are biting, and conversations of eternal consequence are occurring constantly. This is a great work of the Spirit of God. Pray for darkness to be pushed back and lives to be changed forever. There is no endeavor that has higher stakes than the work of investing in people's lives, souls, and forevers. Pray for our leaders who are at the helm of the most important ship in the ocean. Pray for our people who yearn to give their best despite brokenness at every level of life. Pray for those despairing from a magnitude of loss that is almost indescribable. Pray for the church to have her finest hour as Jesus Christ is lifted up and people are driven to Him. **Pray that God sustains our unity, minds, bodies, hands, feet, so we do not dishonor Him.**

Still Betting the Farm on God,

Michael

OCTOBER 22

Two years ago Trinity Church went through "40 Days of Purpose." It was excellent, and many grew, but that time doesn't compare to "50 Days of Katrina." Christian pollsters have asked believers to look back on their lives and identify what has caused them to grow the most. The #1 response was "suffering." We might not want to hear that, but it is often true. It's amazing how this crisis has created simplicity and purity of devotion to Jesus in me.

The Jesus I am encountering is very different from the flannel graph Jesus holding a lamb that I learned about in Sunday school. He is different from the Mr. Rogers figure I met as a teenager, and even the "doctrinally precise" facts of Jesus I encountered in seminary. He is not the political Jesus (have to be part of the right party), social Jesus (His only care is social work), Rambo Jesus, CEO Jesus, or the "nice guy" Jesus.

He is certainly not the Jesus the church has tamed — in Dorothy Sayers's words, *"very efficiently pared the claws of the Lion of Judah, certified Him as a fitting household pet for pale curates and pious old ladies."* The Jesus I am walking with is not boring or predictable. In fact, He surprises me every day, yet invites me to live in His power, presence, and rule. He is inviting me to walk in a Kingdom that is not of this world. It is an invisible Kingdom but is one that is on a collision course with all the kingdoms of this world. Jesus says, *"Start living your life differently; do it My way! Your way won't work. Choose Mine instead!"*

His message is the most compelling thing I've ever heard, and I have a burning desire to invite others into the company of Jesus. Listen to a few notes from people on how this is happening:

"... It became apparent that you and your church had an incredible impact on our lives. To see Trinity rise up out of the ashes of such a tragedy and respond the way you have has changed my personal ministry forever. Even while writing this e-mail, I hold back tears of joy, knowing that God is moving so powerfully through you and Trinity. As a young man looking forward to a life of ministry, I feel beyond fortunate for having stayed just a few days with you. While your congregation might have lost some or all of their physical possessions, they are to me the richest people in all the world. Their daily dependence on God and passionate worship in spite of tragedy is an inspiration that I cannot express in words ... ."

"... I just returned from N.O. working with Urban Impact Ministries ... . The Lord has deeply burdened my heart for the victims of Katrina. I have been consumed with His call to 'give ourselves to the hungry and to satisfy the desires of the afflicted, then your light will shine in the darkness ... to be repairers of the breach and restorers of streets to dwell in!' (Isaiah 58) My wife and I (and four kids) are prayerfully considering selling our home and moving to do full time relief/ministry in some capacity. I don't know what it would look like, but I know the Lord has given me much vision ... . I have such a deep love for the Lord and for people and want to be faithful and obedient as He leads me."

"... I have been longing for the Acts 2 church. Upon coming home, I have been telling everyone I have finally found and got to participate in an Acts 2 church ... . I told one person 'if my life was my own, I'd move in a heartbeat' to join with you all ... . I'm praying that God would show us how we can move into this type of 'doing church' apart from a disaster having to happen."

"After a week at Trinity, it was like Jesus taking my face in the palms of HIS hands, holding my face in front of HIS face to where I could "see" HIM like I never have before. I was looking into the face of a Man whose heart and passion was for people. His face revealed His heart for the lost people today. For a split second His life on earth passed before me ... . His purpose was to seek and save the lost."

Please pray for two things:

1. Pray for the ever deepening needs of people. Some are recovering, some of us are probably not even fully aware of how this is impacting us, and some are desperate. Yesterday, I had to deal with two incidents where people had suicidal issues. The week before, someone wanted to talk to a pastor because her son was threatening to kill her. She wouldn't call the police unless a pastor or priest told her that it was okay. The week before, my secretary looked into her rearview mirror and saw the man in the car behind her hitting his

dashboard. Then he got out of the car and started hitting the hood. She feared he would start hitting her. Some in our congregation have had coworkers and friends commit suicide. These incidents just show the despair that can come from being overwhelmed. Pray for the ministry of comfort that comes from the Comforter.

2. Pray for us to be alert against the schemes of the devil. I told my wife last week that the devil will not let zeal get into a congregation without him trying to steal, kill, and destroy. Sure enough, I sense his attacks. Pray for us to be strong and courageous. Pray we do not wilt in our resolve to persevere for Christ. I have received three separate reports of churches that have chosen to get out of the relief business and get back to church as normal. Maybe that is God's calling, but I fear there will always be a drift to comfortable.

   Pray for us that we will listen and obey God's callings, even when they are hard. Pray we will continue to serve Christ as we serve our community. Pray for hundreds of decisions that need to be made to sustain outreach and in-reach. Pray we remember always our first love, Jesus.

I continue to be a wide-eyed dreamer that the church can change the world. This is happening, one person at a time. The risen Jesus of Revelation 1 is the Lion of Judah Who makes us more than conquerors. Thank you for your support, encouragement, and prayers. I daily experience the feelings of Luke 24 when the disciples said, *"Were not our hearts burning within us while He was speaking to us on the road."* I rejoice in being part of the fellowship of the burning hearts.

Betting the Farm on God,

Michael

OCTOBER 29 **The Backside of the Hurricane**

This week one of the team members told me about one of the families that were helped a few days ago on the Pearl River near Slidell. The family decided to ride out Katrina in their sturdy, raised home. Despite the ferocity of the hurricane, they thought that they had thankfully survived. The violence of the storm subsided, and they went outside to enjoy the calm and survey the damage. For a few moments they experienced euphoria, but that soon gave way to fear. They realized that they were in the "eye," and the backside of the hurricane was coming with vengeance. The water started rising a foot every few minutes. Soon their boat tied to the lower level was up 12 feet or so, and they needed to get in it fast, or the water would overtake their home. In the middle of the hurricane, they maneuvered up the river. The only problem was, when they got to the first bridge, the water was almost bridge high, and the boat could not go under it. So, they docked at the bridge and got onto the bridge. After a few minutes they noticed something big coming downstream. It was their house! It shattered into a million pieces at the bridge. They realized that the water would soon be over the bridge. Their only hope was a mad dash to the boat and try to maneuver to the other side of the river and onto a sturdy looking tugboat. As they got close, they didn't know if it was possible to make it.

They can't explain the last leg of the journey, but in their words, *"God got them on that tugboat, and they rode out the storm."* The man said, *"I never thought about God before Katrina, but now I think about Him all of the time. I have been in church every Sunday since."* I ask you, if a hurricane gets a man connected with God, was the hurricane God's justice or His mercy?

I tell you that story to ask you not to forget us because the backside of the hurricane is coming. If you hear reports of progress (and there is some), the truth is we are only in the eye. The rest is coming, and I sense the water is rising a few feet every day.

1. Some churches have been shut down or badly hurt. One church staff person reported that out of a church

of 127, they had been able to talk to only two people. The rest were scattered. One man told me that their church attendance was down by 2,000 (not a misprint).

2. Counselors have written me to warn me to watch for post-disaster stress syndrome. Another reported the statistics on divorce one year after a disaster are off the charts.

3. Greater numbers of people are dealing with discouragement, sickness, and weariness.

4. Many report to me the guilt they experience. "False guilt" from my perspective. Some feel guilty that they aren't serving more. Others feel guilty because they didn't get hit as hard as someone else or that they still have their job.

5. The newspaper reports daily the next round of corporate layoffs, how broke the city and state are, or who is blaming whom today.

6. Many are simply sick of the debris. Others are mad at FEMA or have the headache of fighting the insurance companies.

Yes, the backside of the hurricane is coming, and it will be worse than the first wallop.

Why the information? Simply a call for you to not forget us and a call to pray. I am making a habit of Asking, Seeking, and Knocking (Matthew 7: 7). I ask you to do the same.

Pray for:

Marriages   Teenagers   Children   Jobs   Strength

Spiritual breakthroughs   A church that is weary

Elders/deacons/staff   Unity   Wisdom   Revival

God is answering prayer. The stories still come in daily.

1. I met a new man at church on Wednesday night. A team had removed a large number of trees from his property that day, and he showed up at service to give thanks. I asked him if he had a home church. He said, *"No, but I'd like to make Trinity my home."*

2. Our free store still operates. There is a continual stream of guests who get food and hear about the Good News.

3. The police headquarters called this week. Many of the officers have been working such long hours that they haven't been able to dig themselves out. They wanted to know if we could help. The answer was *"yes."* That's why we are running teams.

4. Mark Lewis, along with his wife and three young children, is moving from Pennsylvania to Louisiana within a few weeks. Mark will head up the ministry of teams. Amazing. An engineer/project manager gives up the "good life" to come to the disaster. Crazy, yet the Bible says, *"If you save your life, you lose it, but if you lose your life for Jesus's sake and the gospel, you find it."*

5. Today I bumped into a guy I haven't seen in four to five years. I didn't recognize him, but he reminded me of the one time we met. It was through a mutual friend. He told me that friend (whom I hadn't seen in a long time) was not attending church anywhere. I sensed a "divine appointment." I got the phone number and took a shot. It was a "God thing" — perfect timing. He said his whole family had been thinking this week about coming to Trinity. **Yea, God**.

I hope you can tell we are moving forward, though we limp. We see His grace in the midst of our weakness. We identify with Paul's words in 2 Corinthians 4: 7 - 18:

"But we have this treasure in earthen vessels, so that the surpassing greatness of the power will be of God and not from ourselves; we are afflicted in every way, but not crushed; perplexed, but not despairing; persecuted, but not forsaken; struck down, but not destroyed; always carrying about in the body the dying of Jesus, that the life of Jesus also may be manifested in our body. For we who live are constantly being delivered over to death for Jesus's sake, that the life of Jesus also may be manifested in our mortal flesh. So death works in us, but life in you. But having the same spirit of faith, according to what is written, 'I believed, therefore I spoke,' we also believe, therefore also we speak, knowing that He Who raised the Lord Jesus will raise us also with Jesus and will present us with you. For all things are for your sakes, so that the grace which is spreading to more and more people may cause the giving of thanks to abound to the glory of God. Therefore we do not lose heart, but though our outer man is decaying, yet our inner man is being renewed day by day. For momentary, light affliction is producing for us an eternal weight of glory far beyond all comparison, while we look not at the things which are seen, but at the things which are not seen; for the things which are seen are temporal, but the things which are not seen are eternal."

Thank you for not forgetting us!

Betting the Farm on God,

Michael

NOVEMBER 5 **Empty Nest/No Nest/Messy Nest/No Nest**

As I write this letter, it is hard to process all that has happened in recent days. One week prior to the hurricane, we dropped our only child Jonathan off at Baylor University in Waco, Texas, to begin his freshman year. We experienced the "Empty Nest." A week later we fled Katrina and found ourselves as refugees in Birmingham, Alabama. We experienced "No Nest."

Tonight I write from the "Messy Nest." Internal construction of our home is under way. Five rooms and a hallway are being repaired because of water damage after a tree hit our home. Furniture has been moved into a small area, and a large electronic scaffold is sitting in my living room. The carpet has been removed, the walls and ceiling are being repaired, and dust is everywhere. We anticipate that we will need to move out during the reconstruction phase, leaving us once again with "No Nest."

Despite all of this, God's hand is powerful and unmistakable:

1. On Wednesday, a young woman, maybe 20 years old, came into the office and said, *"I want to pay my tithe."* We didn't quite understand, so she explained, *"My church in New Orleans was totally destroyed. This morning I said to God, 'The first church I see, I am going to give them my tithe.' So, I was coming down Hwy. 190, and I saw the Free Food/Free Water Trinity sign, and I came in to pay my tithe."* **God provides!**

2. Later that day a brother and sister drove 1,100 straight miles from Wisconsin to Trinity. They heard about a need we had to house key staff volunteers and decided to donate their fully-furnished travel trailer to us. With joy they dropped it off and headed home. **God provides!** (A staff member is very glad to not have to sleep on the worship center floor every night with all of the team members who have come to serve.)

3. Today, a man came down with a beautiful new truck with a sign on it saying, *"Trinity Disaster Relief."* We have been needing transportation for longer-term volunteers. He gave us the new truck. **Amazing! God provides!**

4. One of the team members said today, *"I've grown more in 3 days than I have in the last five years. It's all because of the people at Trinity Church."* **God provides!**

5. God has opened up opportunities through radio to tell the story of what God is doing in New Orleans. This has included three national radio programs broadcasting from the Moody Broadcasting Network in Chicago, a radio station in Ohio, and one in St. Louis. A Milwaukee newspaper is also writing a story on Trinity Church. These are great opportunities to tell about the real needs of New Orleans and recount the deeds of the Lord. **God provides!**

6. On Wednesday, Pastor Doug Anderson of Bethel Evangelical Free Church in Fargo, North Dakota, flew down to speak at our mid-week service and to lead a staff retreat. Bethel's elders commissioned their senior pastor to care for me and our staff in any way that would help. It was perfect timing! **God provides!**

7. Teams of great servants continue to stream in from all over the United States. Trinity will be up to 120 workers by the end of the week, and more will be working out of Castle Rock Church in New Orleans. **God provides!**

8. A ministry called "Music for the Soul" has recorded seven songs for a new CD to minister directly to those who went through the devastation. They will hold their first New Orleans concert at Trinity on November 20 at our Sunday services. They will be giving out 500 free CDs. **God provides!**

9. President Bill Hamel of the Evangelical Free Church of America will speak at Trinity on December 11. **God provides!**

Please pray for all we have to juggle at this time:

1. House repair

2. Insurance issues

3. Marriage/Jonathan in college
4. New children's building under construction
5. Capital campaign
6. Furnishing a new building (no money for this)
7. Care for the flock
8. Team ministry in the community
9. Leading ever-expanding staff
10. Preaching

Please pray. The needs are great, but the opportunity is greater. Trinity is certainly the target of the Dark Kingdom. I'm certain that my staff each have a target on their backs. **Pray for protection, unity, holiness, and perseverance.**

Pray that our church family and the teams be known as a *"people who have been with Jesus"* (Acts 4: 13). Pray we focus on the size of our God, not the size of our problems. Pray that God builds mighty men and women of God through this suffering. This is an opportunity to put our spiritual roots down deep and hear God call us to a whole new kind of relationship with Him. Once people taste this, most will never want to go back to the old way. It is happening.

Personally, I wouldn't wish this catastrophe on anyone, but likewise, I wouldn't trade what God has been teaching me for anything. I am getting to walk with Jesus and experience His supernatural presence, power, and provision. Despite being weary, I have a joy beyond what I have ever known. Just as Moses could handle life only so long before he had to go up to the mountain, so I am discovering the refreshment of meeting with God. I can do all things through Christ who strengthens me. I love the heart of Paul in Philippians 3: 7 - 14, *"But whatever things were gain to me, those things I have counted as loss for the sake of Christ. More than that, I count all things to be loss in view of the surpassing value of knowing Christ Jesus my Lord, for Whom I have suffered the loss of all things, and count them but rubbish in order that I may gain Christ, and may be found in Him, not having a righteousness of my own derived from the Law, but that which is through faith in Christ, the righteousness which comes from God on the basis of faith, that I may know Him and the power of His Resurrection and the fellowship of His sufferings, being conformed to His death; in order that I may attain to the resurrection from the dead. Not that I have already obtained it or have already become perfect, but I press on so that I may lay hold of that for which also I was laid hold of by Christ Jesus. Brethren, I do not regard myself as having laid hold of it yet; but one thing I do: forgetting what lies behind and reaching forward to what lies ahead, I press on toward the goal for the prize of the upward call of God in Christ Jesus."*

Betting the Farm on God,

Michael

NOVEMBER 11 **Katrina Fatigue**

It's midnight, and as I sit down to write this letter with the television on in the background, the commentator on CNN is doing a story on "Katrina Fatigue." The case was made that Washington has already forgotten about New Orleans and has moved on to other events: Iraq, tornadoes, elections, deficits, etc. Politicians aren't so sure that they want to fund a levee system or help New Orleans in ways that were initially promised. The newly coined phrase is "Katrina Fatigue."

I write to you tonight confident that our network of volunteers and partners has not been affected at all by "Katrina Fatigue."

1. Tonight I spent two-and-a-half hours with 120 volunteers who are being deployed from Trinity. These servants of Christ are fired up, dedicated ambassadors of Christ. Their work ethic is extraordinary, and their compassion is unmistakable. We are most blessed because of the "Katrina Faithful."

2. Many people shared tonight how God was profoundly transforming their own lives as well as others. One young woman told of a struggle she personally had with God. An extended conversation with another woman and an unexpected hug from a team member helped produce a significant breakthrough. It reveals the power of a listening ear and the power of a touch.

3. Another team member reported how their group was helping a member of the community. Some were commenting that the Katrina crisis had not produced recognizable heroes like the firefighters and police in the 9/11 crisis. The local person begged to differ, concluding that church teams are the heroes in Katrina. Wouldn't it be nice if the national news discovered the significance of this phenomenon?

4. I discovered that one man led three different individuals to Christ, and many groups had the opportunity to pray with people in the community.

5. You may recall the dear woman who sent us a $5 gift card despite earning only $130 a week. When I reported this in a Sunday service, someone gave me $100 to send to this dear saint. This week I received a letter back detailing how surprised she was at the donation, but how needed it was. She was totally out of money for her living expenses. God is good. In fact, this woman sent us a new $10 gift card! When I announce this on Sunday, I wonder if anyone will want to bless back this generous woman with the two mites and keep this cycle of blessing going.

6. Trinity received a letter and gift from a man who leads worship at a Christian home. One-third of the participants are in wheelchairs and most are on

Medicaid. He assured me many had very little money, yet their generous hearts produced a check for $550. **What a blessing** from those with so little.

7. One of our work teams has a woman who is blind. Yes, blind! I'm told she goes out and guts homes with the best of them. **Yea, God!**

8. One of the team members noticed a Trinity person come into the worship center and closely eye all of the commotion, look down at the stained carpet, and survey the myriad of sleeping bags. She thought, *Oh my, this woman must be upset with all of the change in the church.* She approached the woman to comfort her. She discovered, rather than being upset, the woman had great joy and was going from spot to spot praying for those represented by the sleeping bags. The "church of the stained carpet" continues on. We have the best people in the world at Trinity. (Sorry, I am absolutely and unapologetically biased on this area.)

9. One team member explained how she was assigned to go door-to-door in New Orleans getting work orders. She was informed that she was in a neighborhood with gangs. A number of young men were sitting nearby, and when she walked by, she quickly realized that they were not just smoking cigarettes. Later in the day, after her team had finished their work in the community, she was walking down the street, and one of the men approached her. He threw his arms around her and gave her a great big hug. He expressed great thanksgiving that someone would unselfishly care for his community. If God can break down walls between gang members and middle-aged women from a different part of the country, can't He do anything?

10. Every day, more and more teams are scheduling to come and make an impact. These teams, who come to give, end up receiving. They find it is more blessed to give than receive and proceed to go back and fire their churches up. **It is a victorious cycle that gets played out day after day.**

I am humbled to serve with people who love God and His bride so much … to serve with people who take risks, pay the price, sleep on floors, ride in stuffy vans, shed the old, embrace the new, understand their callings, celebrate the fruit, and do it all for God's glory.

Rather than "Katrina Fatigue" I think the pattern more closely parallels 2 Corinthians 8: 1 - 5, *"Now, brethren, we wish to make known to you the grace of God which has been given in the churches of Macedonia, that in a great ordeal of affliction their abundance of joy and their deep poverty overflowed in the wealth of their liberality. For I testify that according to their ability, and beyond their ability, they gave of their own accord, begging us with much urging for the favor of participation in the support of the saints, and this, not as we had expected, but they first gave themselves to the Lord and to us by the will of God."*

Betting the Farm on God,

Michael

NOVEMBER 19 **NASCAR Living or Soul Rest**

Writer Dallas Willard states, *"You must ruthlessly eliminate hurry from your life."* This is true because we cannot live the life Jesus intends without entering into the rhythms of life Jesus designed for us. This, of course, is challenging when our lives are a whole lot more like NASCAR than rest.

Just before Hurricane Katrina hit, I got hit between the eyes that my RPMs were set a little too high. Driving across Lake Pontchartrain via the

Causeway to New Orleans one day, I distinctly remember approaching the end of the 24-mile bridge and noticing the speed limit change from 65 to 35 mph. I had a choice — tap the brake or coast. Seeing no other cars around, I decided to coast and let my speed decrease. Within moments I was being waved down by a police officer and was given a ticket for going 22 miles over the speed limit. My 18- year-old son enjoyed hearing every moment of this occasion. He reiterated to me every lecture he had ever received from yours truly. I was reminded several times that he had never had an accident or ticket. He loved to tease me, *"You are supposed to be a pastor."* Even my dear wife, Donna, had a little snicker and some words of instruction. Ouch, yet not the end of the story.

A few days later, our family was traveling to Texas. Donna was driving, and I was asleep in the backseat. All of a sudden I sensed that we were slowing down and heard Jonathan say something like, *"He's coming after you."* Sure enough, a police officer was soon at Donna's window asking her about her speed. She had accidentally missed a sign in this little town. The officer kindly gave her a warning. Of course, my son had a field day with this infraction as well. He loved every minute of this. Pretending to be asleep in the backseat, I confess, I couldn't help at least smile a little … but yet not the end of the story.

A few days after we returned from Texas, I was looking out the window of our home as Jonathan pulled into the driveway. Behind him was … you guessed it, a police car. I walked outside, and the policeman informed me that my son had not fully stopped at the stop sign next to our house. The officer said to me, *"Do you want to give him the medicine, or do you want me to?"* Everything in me wanted to say, *"After all I've been through, you give him the medicine."* Yet I, somewhat begrudgingly, said, *"I will."*

I don't know if these things ever happen in your house, but these things really happened in ours. The men in blue with badges had certainly gotten our attention, and the common thread was, *"Slow down."* Then came Katrina! I have moved at the fastest pace during these past two-and-a-half months than I ever have in my entire life. The needs are great, and the demands seem endless at times. There is a constant juggling of competing time demands in the midst of great opportunities: Pastor/shepherding, community outreach, prayer, preaching, team building, capital campaign, new building, staff oversight, radio interviews, communication, administration, networking, family, etc.

Though my body is occasionally weary, my spirit has been vibrant, fresh, alive, and exhilarated throughout the entire endeavor. I have been working 12-, 14-, 16-, 18-hour days week after week. I was created for such a time as this, and I am amazed by the grace of God, that is unmistakable. The strength I have had to persevere has come from God. Yet, I also hear the Spirit now saying, *"Slow down."* My calling in life is not to be a NASCAR driver, zipping in and out of the lanes of life to gain some elusive checkered flag this world offers. There is a better RPM level that will create a right rhythm for my life and fulfillment of my calling.

As Thanksgiving week approaches, I plan to take a few days off and do three things. Maybe you need to do the same.

1. Pull over

   Jesus said, *"Come to me, all who are weary and heavy laden, and I will give rest ... for your souls"* (Matthew 11: 28, 29). Jesus is saying, *"God is not pro-exhaustion."* I am going to pull over and take some time for:

   Solitude
   Sleep
   Wonder
   Thanksgiving
   Recreation
   Revitalization
   Good food — turkey and pumpkin pie
   Time with family and friends — Jonathan is coming home Wednesday.
   Yea!

   I am choosing to pull over for a time and tune up for the next leg of a very important journey. Do you need to do the same?

2. Pop the hood

It is always good to pray, *"Search me, O God, and know my heart."* —Psalm 139: 23

Fast people, from time to time, need to pop the hood and ask good questions. I got a good list of questions from Mike Breaux yesterday to contemplate:

What's making me idle so fast?
What am I chasing?
What am I running from?
Why is my body running so rough?
Why is my mind constantly racing?
Why can't I say "no?"
Am I addicted to approval?
What is fueling my competitive drive?
What part does procrastination and clutter play in my life?
What part does perfectionism play in my life?
Why am I a perfectionist?
Why do I work so hard to be accepted when I already am?
Why do I work so hard to be someone when I already am?
Why do I feel distant from you, God?
Why, when Jesus says, *"Come,"* won't I?

Great questions, aren't they? Many of these questions don't apply to us, but maybe some do. Those of us who at times suffer from the "Hurry Syndrome" should not be afraid to ask them.

3. Change Lanes

I am choosing to build greater sanity into my schedule. I have finished the "first response" stage of Katrina and now need to enter into a rhythm of life that will sustain me for the entire race. It will be a 500-mile race for sure and will go on for several years. Pray for wisdom as I plan for a new rhythm for my schedule in the coming months. As Rick Warren puts it, I need to Divert daily, Withdraw weekly, and Abandon annually.

How about you? Are you hearing the same words of the Spirit to *"Slow down?"* Have you been driving far too long in the fast lane, swerving and honking through life? Author Richard Swenson helps Americans see ourselves as he writes, *"Take a look at our lives. We send packages by Federal Express, have a long distance company named Sprint, manage our personal finances on Quicken, schedule our appointments on a Day-timer, diet with Slim Fast, and have swimming trunks by Speedo."* That says it all! If your life is like mine … Pull over, Pop the Hood, and Change Lanes!

Prayer:

Lord Jesus, we know that living at NASCAR speeds continually

- *Causes our hearts to grow small and our joy levels to diminish*
- *Causes a heaviness of heart, a weariness of body, and an inner erosion of strength*
- *Causes us to skimp on prayer and causes us to miss the still, small voice of God*
- *Causes our relationships to be superficial and our families to be crippled*
- *Causes soul fatigue, worry, exhaustion, and feelings of always being behind*

Jesus, help us to ruthlessly eliminate hurry from our lives. Help us to enter into the life of Jesus by entering into the ways and rhythms of Jesus. Jesus, we choose to come to You and find rest for our souls, thanksgiving for our hearts, awe and wonder in our minds, and the joy of the Lord as our strength. We choose to live under the rule and reign of God in our life. Amen

Betting the Farm on God,

Michael

P.S. The traffic court D.A. dropped my speeding ticket because it was a first offense. Isn't GRACE amazing in all its forms — big and small?

NOVEMBER 26 **Thanksgiving**

It was Thanksgiving, and Snoopy was sitting on his doghouse. He was upset because Charlie Brown and his family were in the house celebrating with a huge turkey dinner. Snoopy was stuck in the doghouse with dog food. He reflected upon this and said, *"It could be worse ... I could have been born a turkey."* What true words, *"It could be worse."*

Robert Hughes, in his book *The Culture of Complaint*, writes, *"We live in a society where people perceive themselves as entitled to have all desires fulfilled. When that doesn't happen, we see ourselves as victims. It is the culture of complaint."* It sure is easy to expect more and more and more and experience less and less and less of good old fashioned gratitude and thanksgiving. I don't want to miss out on this opportunity this special Thanksgiving week.

I love the story of Jesus in Luke 17: 11 - 19. Remember ten lepers got healed, yet only one made a U-turn and went back and expressed gratitude. It made all the difference in the world to Jesus. He said, *"Where are the other nine?"* Reading between the lines, I think he was saying, *"I wish they would have come back."* Surely they felt thanksgiving, but they didn't express it.

This year I am overwhelmed with gratitude for the amazing grace of God. I cherish my wife Donna and son Jonathan. I am overwhelmed with thanksgiving for my family and friends. These past three months I have seen miracle and miracle. Here are a few more accounts. You may find it hard to believe so many stories are happening, but I assure you these are true:

1. Last week we had someone contact us at Trinity Church asking if we could use a church organ. That was an incredibly generous offer; however, we are more of a praise team-style church and couldn't use the organ.

Following the call, someone walked into our free store. The woman was a pastor's wife from the little town next to ours. Her husband had died in the aftermath of the hurricane, along with two other family members. Their church suffered from Katrina, and she casually mentioned what they really needed was ... Guess … An organ! That led to a time of praise like you wouldn't believe. These new friends were "praising God" just like they did in Acts 2. God is God, and He cannot be stopped or contained.

2. You may remember the dear saint who made $130 a week (with no hope for advancement) who sent us a $5 gift card. After mentioning this generosity to the Trinity family, someone gave me $100 to pass on to this woman. I sent the money to her, and in her thank-you letter, she indicated that she was totally out of money and this $100 was God's miraculous supply. This time she sent us a $10 gift card to be used in the relief efforts.

   I mentioned this to the family at Trinity this past Sunday, and after the service people kept putting $20 bills in my hand, saying, *"Send it to the $5 lady."* By the end of the second service, I had $1,040 in my pocket. You can't out-give God. In Genesis 12 we are reminded that God blesses us so we can bless others, and the whole world gets blessed in the process. I would love to see the expression on the face of this new friend when she opens up the envelope. I'll keep you posted on what God does next.

3. At our services we normally have a sharing time before Thanksgiving. What a thrill it was when a member told how she had shared Christ with her Mom for 10 years, and she just trusted Christ as her Savior!

4. God continues to provide in other astounding ways. Last week we found out that Family Life ministry will put on their Marriage Conference for free right in our town of Mandeville. I talked to the leader of this ministry, and he asked Trinity to help sponsor this early 2006 special conference for hurricane victims. Last Sunday, we had a special concert at Trinity sponsored by Music for the Soul. This team of gifted songwriters and musicians out of Nashville sang for us songs written to those who had been through Katrina. A couple of days ago, I found out that Franklin Graham will be in our area in March and would like Trinity to join with other churches to sponsor a crusade. On December 11, Bill Hamel, President of the Evangelical Free Church of America, will speak at Trinity. These are all gifts from God.

I trust you had a wonderful Thanksgiving. I appreciate your prayers, friendship, and partnership with us in New Orleans.

Betting the Farm on God,

Michael

DECEMBER 6 **Weary, Yet Getting Excited in Louisiana**

Anyone that really knows me knows that I love the Christmas season. There is not much I don't enjoy — the sights, smells, and sounds of Christmas; glittering trees; the squeals of children's excitement; good food; giving of gifts; traditions; extra time with friends; the opportunity to re-establish ties and reminisce with family; and the message of the Christmas story where I am reminded, *"I matter to God."* I love all of that, and usually my sense of anticipation starts early. However, I think my internal calendar has been off a little bit this year, and my expectation for Christmas didn't start being turned on until this last Sunday. This may have been for several reasons:

1. Maybe I'm just kind of weary from the workload.

2. Maybe it's because I haven't really operated off a calendar in three months. It's hard to believe that Thanksgiving is over and December is here.

3. Maybe it's because my home is still a wreck with construction, painting, trees being cut down, and piles of debris lining the road in front of my house awaiting FEMA to pick it up. There are no decorations up, only dust.

4. Maybe it's because my parents recently moved to a distant place and I no longer will return to my boyhood home and the place I celebrated Christmas for the last 43 years. Christmas plans are still up in the air.

Yet, last week, a suggestion from one of my staff members started to change my perspective and get me thinking about Christmas. Tuesday night I made a mental note that at my Wednesday staff meeting we needed to start planning for Christmas at Trinity. When I arrived early on Wednesday, our bookkeeper Liz had already stopped by the church even though it was her day off. She thought she had a stirring from God the night before and told a staff member to pass an idea on at our staff meeting. If it was from God, we could use it; if not, we were to discard it. The staff loved the idea! I sensed it had the fingerprints of God all over it and expressed the outrageously generous heart of Jesus.

The idea was to purchase 370 $50 gift cards from Wal-Mart and have them available in envelopes on Sunday morning to give to Trinity members. Trinity members would then pray and ask the Holy Spirit to prompt them whom to give the cards to. In this way, the Trinity family would be empowered to go out in the name of Jesus and express the love of God to someone who was needy or needed encouragement. People could be creative if they wanted to and buy a turkey for someone, or buy

Christmas presents for needy children. If they wanted to, they could cook a meal and invite someone over to express love at Christmas. Others might just give the gift card to someone to select what is needed.

For me, the Sunday service was energizing and thrilling to watch teenagers and families pick up an envelope. Some immediately knew whom to help, and others would wait on the Lord for direction. Each person was given a blank letter to record the story of how God used the free gift. I can't wait to hear! I am ready for Christmas now. Jesus was right. It truly is more blessed to give than to receive.

Betting the Farm on God,

Michael

P.S. Many thanks to the churches and individuals who have given to us so we could purchase the gift cards to help the needy this Christmas. You are appreciated. Please pray this week that Trinity people will have 370 divine appointments!

This is where the work stopped — temporarily — on the new children's ministry building at the end of August 2005.

I think my new motto should be *"Unless God Shows Up, I am in Big Trouble."* We remain a group of Christ followers in over our heads. Conditions in the New Orleans area are still excruciatingly painful for many. I don't know one person, not one, who isn't up to their eyeballs in stress, pressure, and the demands of life. I can identify — between pastoring and relief work, my days are full. Donna has the unending (so far) task of coordinating painters, construction workers, and tree guys and fighting the insurance company. Yet, we are learning, or in some cases, trying to learn, to moment-by-moment depend on the Holy Spirit.

He continues to be faithful, often in ways that cannot be explained apart from the supernatural.

1. A man named Steve prayed in the Trinity office for maps of Slidell. A few minutes later a work team returned to the church office. *"Hey, as we were leaving the work place today, a guy gave us 10 maps of Slidell. Anyone need them?"*

2. Gene from Montana needed certain tools. A few minutes later someone walked in with the exact tools.

3. A fireman from Illinois wanted to bring a "Sawzall" to Trinity with their team. They didn't have one. The next day he was driving down Main Street and found one in the middle of the street. Apparently, it had fallen from a truck. He put an ad in the lost/found section of his local newspaper, but since it wouldn't appear in the paper for a week, he figured that God was letting him borrow the tool for a week to use in Louisiana! When he got back from Trinity, the owner of the tool called and came to pick it up. When he heard the story of how his Sawzall was used in Louisiana, he was delighted. He gave the fireman $20 and told him to send it to Trinity. He was

amazed his tool went to help with Katrina. If you don't know what a Sawzall is, don't worry; neither do I. However, I rejoice in God.

4. A pastor gave me this account:

There was a 16-year-old girl named Elizabeth. Her family was completely wiped out by Katrina. She came in with her dad and her sister. Their home was gone. She had no clothes. And so, she was taken to a team that helped her get some shirts, but there were no pants there. A woman who was working there said, *"My daughter gave me a pair of pants when she heard that I was coming to New Orleans, and I'll give them to you."* They were just the right size.

And then this woman Karen looked at the girl's feet and saw that she had no shoes. She had a pair of sandals that had been ruined by all the muck, but no shoes. Karen asked Elizabeth, *"What size are your feet?"* They were the same size as Karen's feet, so Karen took off her boots. She had a really cool pair of boots. She knelt down and took a basin and a towel, and she washed the feet of that 16-year-old girl. Then she said, *"Here, you take my boots."*

Elizabeth knew that the workers were church people who were there working in Jesus's name, and she said afterwards, *"I am an atheist."* The workers told her, *"That's okay. Atheists need shoes, too."*

5. At our Wednesday night sharing service, it was our delight to hear one of the team leaders tell about leading someone to Christ on Wednesday. Later, the young man sitting next to him got up and shared the revolutionary things that Christ had been doing in his life. He got out of jail six weeks ago. He clearly

communicated that while he was in jail, he had passed from darkness into the light through the power of Jesus Christ. He was so excited to be a new creation in Christ. Prior to his salvation, he says that he never would have served anyone. Now in the Lord, he was finding great joy in serving others in our community. His heart's desire was to return to this area early next year and serve again. Pray for Tom, that God continues to do great and mighty things through him.

6. Many of you have interacted with Jenn, who coordinates all of the teams who come to Trinity. Jenn shared recently how she has learned to trust God for His supply of cooks for the teams. She told about how at first a man from Texas named Jay came out of nowhere to cook for us. Jay said, *"I have to leave next Wednesday,"* and Jenn said, *"No, you can't leave."* Everyone was wringing hands, saying, *"No, you can't leave."* Jenn was told, *"Don't even worry about it. God is going to give us cooks. You just believe it. God will give us cooks. You just believe it. It's God's deal."*

After Jay left, Crystal came, and then God provided another and another. By then, Jenn had it in her job description to schedule cooks. Last week she wondered who would cook. Thursday, no time to look. No cook coming next week. Friday, no time. Saturday was her day off. She thought the world would not stop revolving if she took her day off. Sunday, no cook. Sunday afternoon Jenn played the piano and had a quiet time with the Father, and God provided a peace that He would provide a cook.

Sunday evening Jenn was calling churches to confirm some information and had temporarily forgotten the need for a cook. She contacted a Virginia church and got the information she needed, and the person said,

> *"By the way, we have a guy who would love to cook."* Jenn replied, *"Of course you do."* The cook was at Trinity the day he was needed. Jenn says, *"This is God's gig, not my gig. It wasn't my job to figure it out, only to put it on the calendar."*

I love what God is doing! He is awesome! So far we have had about 1,200 volunteers work out of Trinity from 15 to 20 states and Canada, resulting in about 40,000 total volunteer work hours. Please know that you can always check our webpage at www.trinitychurchonline.net for updates, and you may want to look at the pictures of our new building that is now scheduled to be completed by April 1 (no joke).

Betting the Farm on God,

Michael

DECEMBER 20

Michael asked me to share a few thoughts this Christmas season:

Merry Christmas to each of you! It's hard to believe that Christmas is in less than a week. I guess that's because we really didn't have a fall here. Did we really have a September - November?

This has been a long year, but God has been faithful. We have been blessed with friends and family who have shown their love in so many ways! Thank you so very much for your kind words, support, and especially your prayers.

When we took our only child Jonathan to college on August 17, I totally expected that the "empty nest" was going to affect me greatly. I was preparing to lead a women's Bible study by Beth Moore entitled *Believing God.* I can remember sitting in a hotel room after we dropped him off thinking about how I needed to believe God's promises now that I had released my son to college life. Little did I know that in less than six days we would be preparing to evacuate our home and our lives would be forever changed. I would now also be "Believing God" for what He could do in and through our lives as a result of Hurricane Katrina. God has shown His faithfulness over and over since August 29. I continue to be amazed. This year has not been easy. I have shed many tears. We have all been weary, but I know that we have a God who never allows anything to happen in our lives without His knowledge. When we got back into town after our evacuation, we stayed a night with friends who had a generator. In the morning I saw an open Bible on the table and tried to read these words:

"God is our refuge and strength, a very present help in trouble. Therefore we will not fear, though the earth should change and though the mountains slip into the heart of the sea; Though its waters roar and foam, though the mountains quake at its swelling pride. ... The Lord *of hosts is with us; the God of Jacob is our stronghold. Selah."*

God is our stronghold. Thanks be to Him for His unspeakable gift of Jesus Christ. May each of you have a very Merry CHRISTmas (and I'm not afraid to say it)!

Love to all,

Donna,
as well as Michael, Jonathan & Fluffy (the dog)

DECEMBER 24 **2005 Katrina Year-End Report — Yea, God!**

I know that some of you love to be told hard numbers and facts, so here is our report as of 12/10/2005 after three months of Christ-centered labor:

Volunteers 1,309
Man-hours 51,498
Work orders 1,069
Work orders done 487
Work orders not started 550
21% of churches have sent four or more teams
52% of churches have sent two or more teams
Volunteers have come from 29 states and Canada

I know some of you love stories of God, so I will include a few:

1. One of the teams got to help Angie with her home in New Orleans. Angie is black, and the team members were white. Angie said her only experience with white people was to see them shooting at her neighbors … until the team showed up. Isn't it great that walls can come down and love can be shown? Angie showed up at church Wednesday night, and we rejoiced with her.

2. One team was so impacted by the team ministry in the community that they said they were going back home and organize their own Compassion ministry.

3. One woman said to me, *"I have no hope."* She lived right near the church, with a home devastated as well as many family issues. Her words were understandable. The next day a team was at her house. She was at the Sunday service and now sees things changing in her life.

4. One person said, *"I just want to end my life."* Please realize how many people are saying these words. Pray for them. Showing practical love and praying with people makes a huge impact.

5. We received an e-mail the other day from a group of churches in Czechoslovakia. They heard about Katrina and our plight and took up an offering for us and sent it. This is a modern day retelling of 2 Corinthians 8 - 9. The generosity of God's people is amazing.

6. Here is an e-mail I got from a brother in Christ at Trinity after telling him I was going to spend a week at Christmas with my family. It shows the awesome kind of people we have at Trinity who are sold out to Jesus and want to take up their cross and follow Him:

Where you are going
I hope the air is crisp
The fire is warm
The company is enjoyable
Your battery is recharged
Your spirit is overflowed with rejoicing
And you can't wait to come back and help us set impossible goals for recovery, renewal, and revival, then push us like heck to achieve them.

7. Remember the $50 gift cards we gave out at Trinity the last two Sundays to empower our membership to go out in the name of Jesus and bless hurting people? We purchased 370 cards and gave out about 330. A couple of days later, Grace Community Church in Columbia, Maryland, called me and said, *"We purchased 360 $50 gift cards and will bring them to you on December 18."* Amazing. We give out gift cards, and God replenishes them so that we can give them out again. **The Manna Principle!**

8. Stories are being written how the gift cards are making a difference. Here are a few:

"My daughter and son-in-law took in a homeless person. Their budget is rather tight, and I sent them this card to help with groceries. They live in Virginia, and the person they helped was a 59-year-old woman from Louisiana."

"Took two cards and gave them to two different single mothers, one who doesn't even have a job. They both cried and wanted to know where Trinity Church was. I invited them to attend."

"... is in her mid-twenties and remarried four months ago after a very bad first marriage. I have witnessed to

her for two years. Three weeks ago, she confirmed that her new husband was/has been having relations with another for months. She has two small children and no family in the area. This card gave her a renewed view of Christian love and caring no matter what your 'holiness' is. Maybe soon she will give her life to God."

"My mom and I both took a Wal-Mart card. I didn't know who I would give it to. I didn't want it to be someone I thought of. I wanted it to be someone God wanted to have it. I prayed for God to put someone in front of me. I talked to my friend I had not spoken to in awhile, and she told me she was going through a divorce. She has four children and had not bought one present yet because her husband won't work and continued to spend their community money. I told her how I had been praying for God to show me a person in need of a $50 gift card donated by my church, and she was the one. She got very emotional and said all I can say is 'thank you.' I told my mom the story, and she wanted to give hers also. Thank you, Trinity."

9. Here is a story from our Trinity Mother's Day Out (MDO) Director:

"I wanted to let you know how God is blessing the MDO program in so many ways. It is truly answered prayers! For the past few months, there have been some ups and downs in running MDO. We hit a real low at Thanksgiving time when I had no teachers working, and it was just me. It was not easy to keep the faith in Him at all times. I was constantly praying for God's help and asking others to pray for MDO, as well. My human side was trying very hard to keep things running smoothly. But I just finally put everything in God's hands. I said, 'God, I will be your servant leader,

but, You are running the show.' Well, it's all about God's timing (not that I didn't already know this!). Almost overnight, He blessed our program with three new teachers. One of our new teachers lost everything in St. Bernard, and now she is buying a home in St. Tammany. She was in need of a job while her eight-year-old son attends school. Another teacher lost her home in Lakeview and was in need of part-time work. We've been able to give her a job in the infant room where she can be with her grandson, who will be attending MDO. We have been able to bless several moms who have been displaced by offering a temporary daycare option while they are handling housing issues during the day. It brings such joy to my heart knowing how God has blessed this program and how the program has blessed others. After the holidays we will be opening the infant room with three new children. There will be eight children in our toddler room and eight children in our three- and four-year-old class. I am getting calls every day from moms interested in placing their children in MDO. Since these moms are mothers of preschoolers, I am also inviting them to attend our MOPS [Mothers of Preschoolers] *group at Trinity, and several have expressed an interest in coming. I pray for these moms and their children that they will be able see Jesus's love through us. Hopefully, you may have a chance to visit MDO, so you can see all the wonderful things that God is doing, all in His timing!"*

I hope you can see why I appreciate the Big "C" Church across the world and the little "c" church at Trinity. God's plan for the church was pure genius. There is nothing like the Church when the Church is working right under the leadership of Jesus!

In closing, I wish you all a blessed Christmas. There is nothing like the support of family and friends. I pray you experience in full measure the Shalom of God. This Christmas we can remember that Jesus was the greatest of all "first responders." He chose willingly to be born in the eye of the storm. He experienced danger, hunger, rejection, homelessness, pain, and even death. He left the safety of heaven for the pollution of earth. Why? **To seek and to save!** He died for you and me and gives spiritual and eternal life to all who trust in Him. What a gift! That is Christmas!

Betting the Farm on God,

Michael

The Trinity Worship Center has been
literally split down the middle
to serve the multiple purposes
of free store/sleeping center on the left
and food services on the right.
The room is converted back to a worship center on Sundays.

JANUARY 2 **Amazing Teams**

After returning from a Christmas break in Maryland with my family, I got to meet the other night with two large teams predominantly of college students. The groups were from Fargo, North Dakota, and St. Louis, Missouri. I was reminded what choice people God is sending us and how awesome college students can be.

1. A woman named Dakota illustrates the compassion and zeal volunteers have to serve God in our community. Dakota had to travel quite a distance on Christmas Day to meet with the bus leaving Bethel Church, an EFCA church in Fargo. As she traveled on a country road, her vehicle swerved, spun, and then flipped, leaving her semi-conscious, upside-down, hanging from her seatbelt. She remained there until police arrived. The lead policeman wanted to take her to the hospital because she was disoriented. Dakota maintained she had to catch a bus to do relief work in New Orleans. Rescue workers sensed this mission was important. Since tow trucks weren't available, at least quickly, on country roads on Christmas Day, the fire department was called to help right the flipped vehicle. Twenty firemen responded to the call and enthusiastically got involved in helping get Dakota on the road to catch her bus for a 22-hour drive our way. As Dakota's beat-up vehicle was pulled from the ditch, the firemen promised to call her every 20 minutes as she traveled to Bethel Church to make sure that she was all right. Dakota knew God called her to our mission field, and Jesus provided for her once again on Christmas Day! This is the kind of volunteers we are getting.

2. One of the great things about Bethel Church was that their team was sent by their pastor Doug Anderson not only to serve in the community, but to help preserve

and maintain our building at Trinity. With 80 - 100 team members sleeping and eating at the building every day and ministry going on 24/7, you can imagine the beating it takes. We haven't been dubbed, "the church of the stained carpet" for nothing. While several Bethel teams went out, some stayed behind to clean our carpets and help at the church building! **What a display of love.**

Thank you, Bethel Church. You have a great group of college students. If any of you knows Doug Anderson, thank him for me. God used him a few weeks back in a strategic way and now once again. We promise to keep using the carpet every day, but it looks very nice today! It is our privilege and pleasure to use Trinity Church as a staging area for God to do His work in New Orleans with churches from 29 states and Canada so far.

3. Numbers of college students shared their hearts. One freshman in college recounted how her spiritual life was drifting and now was renewed. Another told how God opened the door to share the gospel, and seeds were planted. Another told how easy it was to share your faith when serving people for free in our ravaged city. It inspired me to hear the zeal and devotion for Jesus in the lives of these college students. **Yea, God.**

4. Please keep praying for our community. Mark Lewis, our Compassion team director, shared about attending a funeral for a family member of someone he befriended here. What stood out to him was that there was no one except Mark at the funeral home. It dawned on him that all the person's family and friends were scattered across the country. **Imagine!** That's what people are facing here. Life is chilling in many ways as people face enormous challenges. Pray for the comfort of God upon this family.

Happy New Year to all of you.

Betting the Farm on God now in 2006
— It was worth it in '05,

Michael

JANUARY 10 **Morbid, Yet Beneficial … for Me**

"He is no fool to give up what he can not keep, to gain that which he can not lose."
—Jim Elliot

"Only one life, 'twill soon be past, only what's done for Christ will last."
— Author Unknown

"What does it profit a man if he gains the whole world and loses his soul?"
— Matthew 16: 26 (paraphrased)

I have a spiritual practice that I enter into annually on January 1 that propels me into the New Year. It is a bit morbid for some, but it is beneficial for me. It is an exercise in counting and remembering the brevity of life. Every New Year's Day, I read Psalm 90. In part this Psalm says: *"As for the days of our life, they contain 70 years, or if due to strength, 80 years … . So teach us to number our days, that we may present to You a heart of wisdom."*

In my Bible I have marked for many years now how many days I have left if I live to be 70 years old. I do the math, and it helps me to remember life is brief, too valuable to waste. The Psalmist says to learn to count by numbering our days. My days are certainly dwindling. Back in 1994, my record reveals I had 12,410 days left to age 70. This January 1, my math tells me I only have 8,030 days to age 70. I may not live another day, of course, but if I live out a normal life span, the Psalmist tells me to remember how short life is in order to make the most of my one and only life on this side. Morbid … I know … but it works for me.

Each January 1, I also evaluate the prior year and put a plan of growth together for the coming year. I enter 2006 with a sense of great anticipation. Life for me is nothing short of amazing. Despite the challenges, God's blessings continue to flow, and my life is rich with family, friends, and opportunities that I cherished. Jesus is more compelling, inviting, and mysterious than ever. The Word of God is this wild, untamable, uncensored, living book that rocks my world and fills me with direction and life. These days I am trying to drink in every moment and seize each day by squeezing out of it all the goodness God intends. The stakes are high, and the ride will be breathtaking at times in 2006. There is nothing like the adventurous life in Christ. I trust you will find the same in this new year.

Pray for our relief effort as we enter into 2006:

1. Our full-time Compassion staff is up to about 16. These are committed, choice servants who have committed three to twelve months to work at Trinity in our Compassion office. What an answer to prayer! Pray for all the transition and training of the new staff. **To God be the glory.**

2. Pray for a follow-up director for our relief effort. I want to fill this position ASAP to capitalize on all the work in the community. Pray as well for a full-time children's pastor or director for our ministry. Does anyone have any recommendations? It is a great opportunity for the right person.

3. Pray for our resourcing of our new facility that is scheduled to open April 1. Katrina has put us way behind in our giving as pledge gifts have not come in. **God is able. Pray.**

4. **Pray for revival.** A young man, 18 years old, was in my office the other day. God has broken him, and he was so eager to trust Christ. It was a work of God. He was in

church Sunday and brought his entire family. The same day he trusted Jesus, another person came into the free store and was led to Christ. This was the person's first opportunity to lead someone to the Lord. I don't know who was more excited — the one who accepted the Lord or the one God used. The answer was probably the angels in heaven who were celebrating.

5. Pray for my staff. Pray for energy and perseverance. They work so hard. You can pray for them by name if you check the webpage at www.trinitychurchonline.net.

6. Our second Trinity-produced DVD of the work will be finished within the week. You can go to our website and request a new DVD.

Betting the Farm on God,

Michael

JANUARY 17 **Dying to Live**

As each year begins, I usually ask God for a verse to focus on during the New Year. The verse this year is 1 Corinthians 15: 31b — *"I die daily."* I don't think I am going to like this verse … honest … . But I think I'll like the fruit. I have been meditating on Jesus's call to die to self.

"If anyone wishes to come after Me, he must deny himself, and take up his cross and follow Me. For whoever wishes to save his life will lose it; but whoever loses his life for My sake will find it." — Matthew 16: 24 - 25

"I tell you the truth, unless a kernel of wheat falls to the ground and dies, it remains only a single seed. But if it dies, it produces many seeds."
— John 12: 24

Jesus is telling me that I need to die in order to really live. This dying begins with:

my ambitions

my rights

my control

my comforts

my hopes

my traditions

my self-interest

my politics

my agendas

my selfishness

my greed

my pride

my self-sufficiency

my image

God demands that real life flow out of abiding in Him rather than from my own strength.

Katrina means "cleansing." I believe that in many ways it has been a cleansing not only for New Orleans but for me. He is shaking things up from top to bottom. He is getting rid of the junk in my life … cleaning house … torching what needs to be burnt. He is stripping away the excess baggage, and I am traveling lighter than I was before. The change has been great, and I'm having to die to certain things and in some cases grieve certain losses. It is amazing to think what has happened in four months.

1. We entered into the empty nest days before Katrina as we dropped Jonathan off at Baylor.

2. For weeks we functioned in total survival mode, making up life one day at a time.

3. We are adjusting to the financial challenges of paying for college, which all of you know is not cheap.

4. Trinity Church has had so many people scatter and many people move away. Being a relational person, this is a challenging dynamic in my life. I estimate 30% of the church family has been dispersed. Thankfully, God is refilling the ministry with many newcomers.

5. I have lost three staff members due to Katrina or God's new directions. These positions need to be filled. Our full-time Compassion staff has swollen to about 16, which positions us to make a huge investment in the community.

6. With my parents moving and encountering their own health challenges, it put me in another season of life.

7. Our new building is coming on line April 1, and a new elder board is coming together for the first time tonight.

8. Our house is still under construction. We are ahead of many, but these projects seem to go on for a long time. Things are so chaotic, I have a cardtable set up in my bathroom, and now I do all my writing and sermon prep there. I'm NOT kidding! This is life in New Orleans.

Change is everywhere, yet all these areas provide an opportunity to practice dying to self. The result is, there is something very alive in me. The Spirit is making a way. God makes streams in wastelands. Jesus brings beauty out of ashes. There may be sorrow at night, but joy comes in the morning. God is the Master at bringing resurrections out of deaths. **Yea, God!**

Is there any area you need to die to? Any area you are grasping and need to let go? Any area you are:

Pushing

Fearing

Pulling

Forcing

Manipulating

Demanding

Clinging

Tired

Grasping

Wound Up

Stressing

Holding Onto

Exhausting

Any area you need to die in order to live?

Betting the Farm on God,

Michael

JANUARY 27 **Bridge Building**

It is an amazing time to be preaching at Trinity Church to our dear people, guests, and teams. Despite so much hardship and heartache, the family of God is so responsive to the Word of God. Last Sunday I preached from Acts 10 on "Bridge Building." In the passage we encountered the beloved disciple Peter, with a great big plank in his eye. His blind spot was a deep-seated prejudice against Gentiles. Peter was brought up this way. The lens of the Great Commission to go to the whole world was simply the Jewish world for Peter. In this he was content and yet blinded to the bigger call of God. We discovered that God was about to do quadruple bypass surgery on Peter through an encounter with Cornelius.

God orchestrated events so that Peter had a choice. He could keep the plank in his eye or die to self. This was a defining moment. If Peter built a bridge, it would cost him — ego, pride, reputation, etc.

You can imagine what friends around him would say if he invited Gentiles into his home. (*"Did you see what I saw?" "What's this neighborhood coming to?" "Pretty soon they'll all be moving in!"*) Peter chose well and went with the Gentiles. I wonder if he thought, *"Hey, these are human beings! Normal guys ... we have a lot in common ... I was wrong ... Why have I been afraid all of these years?"* All of this led to the conversion of Cornelius and his family, but the biggest conversion was the transformation of Peter to be a bridge builder.

It seems like God is still in this transformation business. In our two services about 10 people raised their hands signaling they prayed to trust Christ. In addition, I had a small wooden plank and a pencil put in every bulletin. At the end of the service, I invited people to write on the plank any blind spots to being bridge builders, or lack of love God had revealed to them during the service and then come up and put the plank at the foot of the cross. Person after person made their way up front. Great numbers of people? On the planks were words like: fear, judgmentalism, legalism, prejudice, labeling, pride, ego, and attitude.

Katrina means "cleansing," and that is what God is doing in me and in others. He is cleansing us for His purposes. One man said, *"Michael, you didn't have enough planks for me to write down all of the stuff I needed to."* God was freeing him up one step at a time. As we left Trinity, we were all primed to step out of our circles of comfort, build bridges to those around us, and tell others about our friend and Savior Jesus. Jesus is building His Church in the devastated region of New Orleans.

This reminds me of the guy who told me a little while back about his encounter with a waitress at a restaurant. This Christ follower was with a Christian friend, and the waitress was a young girl with multi-colored hair and piercings in many places. As he put it, *"It looked like she was fishing and her tackle box exploded."* Got the picture? When the girl left the table to get the drinks, this man conveyed his disgust to his friend.

To his surprise, his friend responded, *"Do you believe lost people matter to God?"* Gulp. Uh. Have you been there, too? I have been. When the waitress returned to the table, the friend called the waitress by name and said, *"Is there anything we can do for you?"* The girl with the metal piercings in many places got real tender and said, *"Yes, I'm getting married this coming weekend. Pray that my marriage would last."* What a way to build a bridge. The man telling the story learned a lot about God's heart. God was doing surgery on his heart, too!

I am blown away daily with what Jesus is doing in our midst:

1. I just got an e-mail from the college team from the St. Louis E-Free Church that served over Christmas break (*Hi, Erin and Kristen!*). These zealous young adults discovered the *"power of God through simple service."* They saw the example of ministry through action. On January 29 they will be telling their story to their church and how they desire to start a "compassion ministry" for the neighborhoods surrounding the church. As Kristen puts it, *"I am very encouraged that my church was so moved by a bunch of punk kids who decided to give up their Christmas break to serve. It is quite humbling in this sense, seeing that God used us to inspire my whole, enormous church — to spur them on to something more. Surely God has used the weakest to make the church strong!"*

2. One friend told me he got a wonderful gift for Christmas from his daughters. They knew he wanted to return to Trinity to help. They gave him $200 to handle expenses in Louisiana.

3. One e-mail from a man stated that outside of his wedding day and the birth of his children, the time at Trinity was the single greatest experience of his life and the most fulfilling thing he has ever done. He has a gaping hunger for what's next. **Don't you love it? Do I hear any *"Amens"* out there?**

4. Here are reflections of one team:

"The landscape is stunning: Neighborhood after neighborhood filled with houses, now abandoned, almost all with water lines at least halfway up the walls, parts of roofs missing, sometimes still bearing the red spray-painted markings left by rescue workers in boats, debris still scattered randomly on roadsides and in yards. Trees fallen on houses and cars, still untouched four months later. Cars, trucks, buses — exteriors dented and pierced, interiors fuzzy with mold — parked at crazy angles in odd places or sandwiched together like sticks of chewing gum or wrapped around overpass pillars. Virtually everyone we talked with in New Orleans said they had lost everything.

"The very proposition of our team's work is preposterous. We enter someone's home and go through their drawers and closets and shelves. We drag all their personal belongings and household furnishings out into the front yard, throwing it all into a huge pile. Then we take sledge hammers and crowbars to the walls, systematically destroying the inside of the house, leaving only a skeleton of 2-by-4 studs.

"This is not about houses. This is about people. When you're out in the neighborhoods and you see people, stop what you're doing and approach them. Tell them who you are, why you're there. Listen to their stories. Weep with them. Hug them. Find out how you can pray for them, and then circle up and do it.

"Each member of the Chatham team has left a special mental snapshot in my mind. Lucy approaches a

couple of ladies who are stopping traffic for a heavy equipment operator smoking a cigarette, pulls them all into a prayer circle with the whole team, and we pray with them and for them. One of the ladies declares Lucy a 'woman of God.'

"Emily walks out of a house that we are gutting, sits down, and says, 'This is really emotional.' She and Zach take a walk around the block to talk to neighbors they spot across the back yard and come back exhilarated at having ministered to a total stranger. When we go out to eat one night, Nikki, a waitress herself, notices a waitress who is wearing obvious signs of fatigue and worry and stress, strikes up a conversation, and tries to encourage her. She and Stephanie volunteer to pray in the circle we often form in front of houses.

"Matt and Ron are relentless warriors of grace, quietly leaving behind a trail of simple acts of kindness. Matt gives one of his own tools to an appreciative homeowner, who he knows will need it. As we clean out the vehicles, Ron walks around asking, 'Do you have any trash I can take care of for you?' Saying goodbye, four strapping young college guys from Mizzou surround Ron and squeeze him in a collective bear hug.

"Crossing over Lake Pontchartrain on our last trip out of New Orleans, Matt and I read from Proverbs, talk about our families, ponder the churning waves and the city lights beyond them, and try to comprehend our experience. Honestly, the contrasting images of utter despair and hope offered are still too much for me to take in completely. It's enough now simply to know that God knew this day would come and go and

that, through it all, from the ashes, He is again speaking beauty and grace."

5. I spent Wednesday to Saturday of last week in Minneapolis at a Ministerial Conference with 400 to 500 pastors in the E-Free Church. It was amazing to have so many say they are praying for us and are not going to forget us. What a comfort and joy. I love partnering with churches across our country.

6. We have had teams from 29 states and Canada join us. Last week, we had our first team member come from Paris, France. **Wow! Only God!**

These stories can go on and on. The reason for the stories is … God! I can't explain it all, but God has graciously done something very special. He is doing it, and He deserves the credit!

A few things to pray for:

1. Pray for hurting people in our region who are dealing with the grief, loss, depression, and chaos of living in a devastated city. The suicide hotline in our area used to handle 100 calls a day, and it is now getting 900 a day.

2. Pray for my church staffing needs, especially that God would provide a children's pastor or director and an operations person, ASAP.

3. Pray for the resources to provide furnishings for our new children's building that is scheduled to open April 1. We did not have any money set aside to furnish the building and were planning to run a mini-capital campaign in the fall. Katrina interrupted all of that. I don't know where the funds will come from, but despite my uncertainty on this, I'm betting the farm on God once again.

4. Pray for Mark Lewis, who leads our Compassion staff, and for new leaders for our men's and women's ministry.

Betting the Farm on God,

Michael

FEBRUARY 12 **Signs and Wonders**

"And they were continually devoting themselves to ... prayer. Everyone kept feeling a sense of awe; and many wonders and signs were taking place through the apostles." —Acts 2: 42 - 43

In Henry Blackaby's book *Experiencing God*, his mantra is, *"Find where God is working, and join Him there."* We are trying to do that, and His fingerprints are everywhere.

1. This week a team from Pennsylvania was given the assignment of helping a woman named Georgia. They had a sizable job, considering the devastation of Katrina on this woman's property. They diligently cleared trees and debris but were stopped by an enormous uprooted stump that they were unable to remove with chain saws. While returning to work on Georgia's house on the second day, they got delayed by a raised drawbridge as they were crossing over Lake Pontchartrain. Waiting three cars in front of them was a man with a bobcat. Could that be God's answer? Was this a divine appointment on the middle of the Causeway? Was this attempt foolishness or faith? Who would know unless someone stepped out in faith. A man got out of their vehicle and went up and knocked on this man's window, told him their dilemma, and asked for help. A few hours later he showed up at Georgia's house. At the sight of the size of the stump, he told the team that it was impossible to pull up the stump. The team knew this was a God-thing, and they

said, *"You pull, and we will pray this humongous stump out."* He pulled with the bobcat, and it came right out. **Yea, God!**

A FEMA truck was right down the street hauling away debris. The team raced down the street and said, *"We prayed for you, and here you are."* FEMA came and took all of the debris away from in front of her home. Georgia was presented with a clean yard. Good story? … The best is yet to come. The team got to know and love Georgia. They told her about their friend Jesus. She trusted Christ for her sins. She had been searching for some time. I got to meet her Wednesday as she attended the service. **Yea, God!**

2. On Wednesday night another guest attended. I spoke on the topic of "Why Heaven is Better" from Philippians 1: 21. After the meeting one of the teams got to talking to their guest (they had worked at her home), and she found salvation! Transformed lives are God's greatest signs and wonders. **Yea, God!**

3. A few weeks back, my wife Donna and son Jonathan gutted a home in Abita Springs. The owner of the home has now become Donna's friend, and she is attending Trinity Church regularly. In fact, Wednesday night her son — and uncle, who hasn't been to church in ages — came to the service. The uncle said he'd be back. **Yea, God!**

4. I met with the children's pastor from Hershey Evangelical Free Church this morning. He told about praying for Trinity and the community here and asked God what he could uniquely do to assist in God's work. Immediately after praying that prayer, he received an e-mail from Mark Lewis, our Compassion director, asking

if he could help Trinity with Vacation Bible School this year since Trinity lost their children's director. Bingo! He had his answer, and we met today to start the coordination of his volunteers with those of Trinity.

5. These stories could go on and on. They don't end. Last night I shared with the teams how, in Exodus 17, Joshua was sent into the valley to fight the Amalekites while Moses went to the hilltop to lift his arms in prayer to God. While his arms were lifted high, Israel prevailed, but when his arms drooped, the enemy made inroads. You know the story how Aaron and Hur came alongside of Moses to keep his arms raised, and there was great victory. At the end of the meeting, a pastor brought eight men forward and raised my arms and prayed for me and Trinity. Amazing, yet this is what is happening at Trinity Church.

At times our arms are very tired, yet people from all over the country are praying for us, sending resources and teams. Because of all of you, and the power of God, we are prevailing in the work.

Here are some stats on the groups we have scheduled over the past few months:

Castle Rock

- Teams: 51
- Completed Work Requests: 286
- Outstanding Work Requests: 35
- Volunteers: 785
- Work Hours: 23,230

Trinity Church

- Teams: 153
- Completed Work Requests: 834
- Outstanding Work Requests: 432
- Volunteers: 1,898
- Work hours: 72,810

Sorry I haven't written in the last two weeks, but this only leads to one more story. A few weeks back Donna and I were strong in spirit but weary in body. We went for a walk and commented that it would be helpful if we could get a little break. When we got back to the house, I checked my e-mail. A new friend from a Chinese Bible Church outside of San Francisco asked if we could come and speak at their four services and if possible stay a few days for a little R&R. We took Pastor Steve up on his kind offer and met his wonderful church family. They allowed us to see the area and behold the beauty of God's creation in that area of the country. We returned refreshed, rejuvenated, and thankful. We even look forward to teams of Chinese believers joining with us in the work of New Orleans. **God is good.**

Betting the Farm on God,

Michael

And the work goes on ... at the new Family Discipleship Center next door to Trinity Evangelical Free Church.

FEBRUARY 21 Urgent Request for Prayer and Help for Trinity Church

I am convinced that Trinity Church is where it is today after Katrina because of the prayers of the people of God, like you! We may be weak, limping, and weary, but we are advancing in the cause of Christ and experiencing the sufficiency of His grace for teams, provisions, encouragement, and fruitfulness.

I now need for you to pray for a very urgent need for four staff positions to be filled. During the aftermath of Katrina, I rejoiced that God used the Trinity staff in an extraordinary way. The dedication, camaraderie, zeal, heart, and dependence on Jesus were the best I have ever seen. I tremendously enjoyed my friends on my staff. Many of you have been part of Trinity or Compassion teams and know the wonderful staff members I am talking about.

God, in His wisdom, however, has taken several staff members to new mission fields:

- Steve Olsen, our associate pastor of adult ministries, has just accepted a senior pastor position in a church just outside of Houston.
- Joycelyn Romero, our operations director, secretary, and "everything else" leader has relocated to Austin, Texas, with her family.
- Barbara Oden, our bookkeeper, has relocated to Memphis because of some incredible opportunities in her adventure of faith.
- Suzanne Cole, our part-time children's director, has graciously stepped out of her position to allow a full-time pastor or director to lead our thriving children's ministry. Suzanne felt led by Jesus to do this and is still very active helping us get into our new children's building.

I love each of these people and miss each one. They are choice servants in God's Kingdom. (I guess Texas must be a bigger mission field than Louisiana for God to move so many over there!)

Would you pray for the following four positions to be filled and pass the word to potential applicants to send us a resume? You may know of some seminary students graduating, pastors who are looking for a change, or a talented lay person who would be perfect for the job.

1. Associate Pastor of Adult Ministries
   Trinity Church is a growing, vibrant, grace-centered, Evangelical Free Church of about 700 Christ followers. The candidate must love Jesus and Be a strong leader who is able to lead, train, and motivate volunteers and oversee a wide array of adult ministries spanning small groups, men's, women's, discipleship, and care. This family-oriented community is located on the Northshore of Lake Pontchartrain, where you will find some of the best schools in the state. Better yet, we are experiencing revival, renewal, and an Acts 2 kind of experience in the aftermath of Katrina. A 15,000-square-foot educational building will open in April. If you have been hearing the "still small voice" say *"I've got a new adventure for you,"* please apply.

2. Pastor of Children's Ministry
   Trinity Church in Covington, Louisiana, is a contemporary EFCA church with an average attendance of 700. Of this 700, 140 are children from birth through sixth grade. We are looking for a dynamic, creative, fun-loving person who is passionate about Jesus and able to create environments that are irresistible to children and their parents. The ideal candidate must be able to cast vision, recruit, train, and mobilize volunteer staff. A new $1.5 million state-of-the-art children's building will open in April 2006.

3. Follow-up
   This is a position of assimilation and care that will last over the next year or year-and-a-half to follow up spiritually on the hundreds of contacts Trinity Church

and Compassion teams have had in the community in the aftermath of Katrina. This person will need to equip, envision, and raise up teams to assist in the process of outreach, follow-up, care, and enfolding new people into the local church.

4. Operations/Bookkeeping
 This person will handle bookkeeping and oversee building and grounds, as well as interface with Compassion. We are praying whether this will be a full-time position or two part-time positions.

I preached yesterday on Joshua 14. Caleb at 85 years old said, *"I want to take on the giants in the hill country."* This faithful servant saw an opportunity, not an obstacle; God, not the giants — and chose to walk by faith, not fear. The result was Caleb entered into the Promised Land for the glory of God. At Trinity, we have giants to tackle, mountains to climb, and obstacles to overcome. We have had no other choice than to bet the farm on God. This is one more opportunity to see His provisions and boast in God's faithfulness. Please pray — and send us qualified applicants — and I will keep you informed.

Betting the Farm on God,

Michael

FEBRUARY 24 **Sorrow in the Evening, Joy in the Morning**

There are a lot of stories told and testimonies given at Trinity Church these days. Last night was no exception. A man named Clarence gave praise for the work team from Minnesota that cleared up his home freely, lovingly, diligently, and in the name of the Lord Jesus. Yet, he also revealed his family's tragedy. His missing 22-year-old nephew was found the day before, shot in the head, maimed, and burned. His charred body was found in his SUV. So much pain, yet he stood before us all, giving glory to God and expressing his hope in Jesus even though the funeral was the next morning. **Pray for Clarence!**

The Wednesday before, a member of a work team from Pennsylvania expressed his mixed emotions about New Orleans because of all the negative reports he heard prior to his arrival. He pictured a complaining people with a handout mentality. God placed him in the Ninth Ward for the week, the hardest hit area in New Orleans. (Donna and I saw it for ourselves last week!)

Far from the media's portrayal of the truth, he discovered all week long a people who had lost everything yet were working hard and were hope-filled and praising Jesus though their suffering was great. One man he worked with had been a drug addict prior to Katrina but made a choice in the aftermath to choose the path of honor and care for his family. Katrina was bad, but God is working it for good. He said, *"Michael, you have to get the real story out to what is really happening."* How God is working through this will not be portrayed on your television sets.

Another family graced our doors last week, and they were so moved by the help they got that they arranged for the whole story to be told in a lead article today in the *Times-Picayune* newspaper. The man runs a Girl Scout camp in our town and had a daunting task of acres of clean-up. The man had given up on church and dabbled with Buddhism over the years. At first he was totally skeptical of our team but soon discovered they were as genuine as they come. In the newspaper article he said, *"I'm not a big church person, but I think I've changed my mind. These were really sweet people ... they didn't ask for a thing. I'm not used to that."* The newspaper heading read, *"Ranger is blown away by group's generosity."* Seeds were planted. **Pray for Mike and his family.**

Here is another story from a team member that blows me away. This dedicated servant drove 23 hours to Trinity and then had to turn around two days later to drive 23 hours back home because of a death in the family. She struggled ... *Why, Lord, after just two days?* Here's what she wrote: *"When we returned, we prayed ... and prayed ... and prayed ... seeking answers .... My journal from our trips to Louisiana had one recurring theme ... thank you, Jesus, for allowing me to understand what You truly meant by the 'church.' Thank you, Jesus, for helping me to realize that the church is a family, not a building. When we returned, it became clear that where we live is seriously lacking for ministry. We have to drive 30 miles to [an area] Community Church, as there are no outward focused churches in our area. They are all, as our pastor would say, 'arguing over the color of the carpet.' People are broken, sad, lonely ... and most of all ... hungry for Jesus. We started calling around to look for a group of people to pray about this situation, as there are several local churches currently experiencing fallout. The bulk of the population is either unsaved or in great spiritual need. I pushed ... 'Lord ... I don't want to leave ... I love my church!' It became clear that He was preparing us. Before we knew it, the situation seriously escalated. We started calling on families. We got, 'What are you doing Sunday ... can you meet Sunday?' This Sunday we have nearly 30 people meeting in our living room. Our senior leadership at church is seriously investigating an E-Free church plant in our area. Praise God for the unknown; praise God for the unsaved, as they are future servants of Jesus; praise God for all He is every day."*

I'm undone by this. God is working in such powerful ways, and I hear stories like this every day. One church in St. Louis has started a new ministry in their town after serving for a week at Trinity. Entitled "Simply Service," this ministry is dedicated to reaching lost people for Jesus Christ by doing very specific, unskilled tasks such as raking leaves, cleaning homes, and manual labor. In the process of "Simply Service," God does His work. **Yea, God! Way to go, Kristen and St. Louis E-Free!**

A team from my home church, Forcey Memorial Church in Maryland, returned home after spending two of their days gutting a home without getting to meet the owners, who were still out of the area as evacuees. Upon their return home to Maryland, they got a call from the grateful homeowners who wanted to express thanks. The Forcey team discovered this refugee family was now living in ... Maryland, not far from Forcey. A grand meeting of the team and the family is being planned.

Pray for revival in New Orleans and the Gulf region.

As you can tell from the stories, there is so much pain, yet God is present. There is sorrow at night, but joy comes in the morning. As Paul put it in 2 Corinthians 4: 8 - 12, 16 - 18, *"We are afflicted in every way, but not crushed; perplexed, but not despairing; persecuted, but not forsaken; struck down, but not destroyed; always carrying about in the body the dying of Jesus, so that the life of Jesus also may be manifested in our body. For we who live are constantly being delivered over to death for Jesus's sake, so that the life of Jesus also may be manifested in our mortal flesh. So death works in us, but life in you … . Therefore we do not lose heart, but though our outer man is decaying, yet our inner man is being renewed day by day. For momentary, light affliction is producing for us an eternal weight of glory far beyond all comparison, while we look not at the things which are seen, but at the things which are not seen; for the things which are seen are temporal, but the things which are not seen are eternal."*

Please pray for:

1. The weary. This is everyone, every day. Pray for Donna as she feels the effects of Katrina, especially at this time. The demands on her life are rigorous, and she has many friends moving away, including one very special friend.

2. Pray for our four new staff needs. We are bringing in a candidate for our children's pastor/director position soon. Pray for God's wisdom.

3. Pray for the multitude of decisions we need to make as we bring on a new building, figure out how to pay for the building and furnishings, and reach out to our community. Praise God for the Hershey Evangelical Free Church, which has agreed to co-lead our summer Vacation Bible School with our team.

4. Pray for revival in New Orleans, the Northshore and the Gulf region.

Betting the Farm on God,

Michael

MARCH 4 **Death of the Church is Greatly Exaggerated**

Those of you who know me well know that I am a reader. Over the years, I have profited from and enjoyed the writings of Christian pollster George Barna. He has brought a great body of research and insight to the body of Christ. This is not true, I believe, in his latest work entitled *Revolution.*

In his new bestseller, he expresses great passion for the capital "C" church, the universal group of believers in Jesus, but misses completely the biblical doctrine of ecclesiology or, practically put, the vital importance of small "c" churches around the world. He expresses enthusiasm that there are 20 million people, dubbed "Revolutionaries," who largely operate outside of commitment to a local church. *Revolution* sees believers *"choosing from a proliferation of options, weaving together a set of favored alternatives into a unique tapestry that constitutes the personal 'church' of the individual."* In fact, Barna writes, *"whether you become a revolutionary immersed in, minimally involved in, or completely disassociated from a local church is irrelevant to me (and, within boundaries, to God)."* He illustrates revolutionaries who have eliminated church from their busy schedules because the ministry is not sufficiently stimulating. He is excited about the revolution outside the church and predicts the decline of the local church.

A few reflections:

First, Barna downplays, disregards, or misses the biblical instructions on the central and essential place of the local church in the cause of Christ. Roger E. Olsen writes in *The Mosaic of Christian Belief* (InterVarsity Press, 2002), *"No where in the Great Tradition of Christianity before the twentieth century can one find the uniquely modern phenomenon of "churchless Christians."* The great revivals of the past always brought people into local churches or created new ones.

Second, as a pastor, I am and trust will always be excited about the little "c" local churches, warts and all. I have to be. Jesus loves the church and gave Himself up for her. I must love what Jesus loves. He loves His churches.

Third, the predictions of the demise or decline of the Church are greatly exaggerated. Jesus will build His Church, and the gates of hell will not prevail against her (Matthew 16: 18). The church has survived far darker days than our life in America.

Fourth, leaders need to call believers away from the consumerist and entertainment styles of our day to the radical call of Jesus to "*die daily*." Barna's phrase "personal church" is simply a reflection of "consumer" Christianity and at odds with Jesus's call to community that expresses itself in relationships of commitment rather than convenience.

We need to call people away from the "ecclesiastical buffet" where we constantly pick and choose, hopping churches based on the hottest menu of the day. The Kingdom of God gets confused with the mall. Some think of themselves belonging to multiple churches rather than deeply rooted in one body. In so doing, relational roots remain shallow, and people remain lonely and disconnected.

Fifth, I am a wide-eyed dreamer believing that Jesus is at work in the world and some of the best days are ahead for the church. Even if we are small, He will be faithful to the remnant who possess His Spirit. Rather than "consumers," we come consumed with devotion to Jesus. We realize we don't go to church, but we are to be the Church. Our desire is to come to give rather than get, yet in giving we receive. As Jesus promised, *"Whoever finds his life will lose it, and whoever loses his life for My sake will find it."*

—Matthew 10: 39 (NIV)

Lastly, my experience of the last six months reminds me there is nothing like the local church when the local church works right. Just as in Luke 23, my heart is lit with the "fellowship of the burning hearts" as we see the visible hand of Jesus at work. Jesus has radically touched my heart and many others.

1. Wednesday night during our service, a man said, *"I just want to share that there's been a lot of conversations and debates about 'Why bother?' and 'Why rebuild?' You know, what a senseless thing to have the city*

where it's at in the first place. And it has really touched me because I've got an answer! I feel now a real answer ... because there's people here ... and God loves those people!" **He gets it!**

2. Here's a note I got this week from a member of the church who was helping a woman and kids who were dealing with an arrest and abuse charges in the family: *"I was desperate for help, and the church was the first place I thought of to run to because I have seen these past few months what the church and God's people are doing in His name. Even though her 'disaster' was not directly Katrina-related, the devastation to her life and the lives of her children was the same. Her disaster had the same consequences. She lost everything that she knew was her identity and that of her children instantly."*

Since the woman could no longer afford their house payments, she had to sell the house which was in the middle of repairs that her husband had been working on. The team was able to transform the house, both inside and out, getting it ready to sell.

The note continued, *"She was overwhelmed with grief and all the problems involved in preparing her house for sale. Satan meant to destroy her life and the lives of her children. But the King has one more move. Praise the Living Lord God Who is so faithful. My niece said, 'I had prayed for an angel, and God saw fit to send an army of angels. The hands and feet of Jesus swarmed my house like bees in a hive.'"*

3. I've been surprised every day this week with stories of God's care, provision, compassion, and goodness. There are daily opportunities to share the gospel, and some seem so close to crossing the line. Pray! We see our new building progressing and this week received

plans for the renovation of our old educational wing. Good candidates are emerging in our interview process for new staff. We even have a possibility of getting all or part of a paved parking lot. (This would take a miracle of money, but if God is in it, He will make a way.) Hour by hour Jesus works as Head of the church and watches over His bride.

Rather than read *Revolution*, I have a better idea for Revival and Revolution. Draw a four-by-four-foot square with chalk. Step into it. Proclaim that *the revolution starts here — with me*. Yield to Jesus. Let Him ignite the fire in you, and people will come out and watch you burn. Your local church will be strengthened, and your pastor will rejoice.

Betting the Farm on God,

Michael

MARCH 9 **Important Prayer Requests for New Orleans**

This morning I had the distinct privilege of attending a prayer meeting and luncheon with Billy Graham and his son Franklin in preparation for this weekend's "Celebration of Hope" crusade in the New Orleans basketball arena. It was inspiring watching a courageous, yet feeble warrior come to the pulpit using his walker and aided by his son. With an exceptionally keen mind, he communicated a message of hope. Billy Graham said, *"I'm devastated by what I have felt and seen."* He said he hadn't called his wife because as of yet he was not emotionally capable of doing that. Such is life in our area. Yet, this elder statesman reminded us that, *"Out of disaster will grow a new New Orleans"* because the city needs moral and spiritual renewal. In the midst of our mayor's race (22 candidates), Mr. Graham is praying that God will become the mayor of New Orleans. He reminded us that just as God multiplied blessings on Job, so He will do that for our area. He also said, *"Jesus is no security against storms, but He's the perfect security in the storm."* Would you pray for us this weekend?

1. Pray for Billy Graham's "Celebration of Hope" Saturday night at 7 and Sunday afternoon at 4. Pray for hope to abound and many to come to faith in the Lord Jesus.

2. Pray for our four staff positions to be filled. We have a candidate coming this weekend to be interviewed for our children's pastor position.

3. Pray for Mark Lewis, our Compassion Ministry director. Mark is a choice leader and has been a wonderful friend. Most of our two-to-four-month volunteers are returning home soon, and we do not have people to replace most of them. Would you give one to twelve months to the work? Do you know anyone who can make this kind of commitment? **Please pray.**

4. Pray for many leaders who are weary this week.

5. Pray for our follow-up of many new people who are being reached out to spiritually. Praise the Lord for those who are trusting Christ and getting connected.

Betting the Farm on God,

Michael

MARCH 17 **Lessons I'm Learning Six Months After the Storm**

One of my earliest sets of reflections on Katrina six months ago was entitled "What I Learned Today." I haven't forgotten those early lessons of surrender and faith. Now after a half-year, I can say that Jesus continues to teach me lessons in the arena of faith. The scripture and my own journey reveal God's ways:

1. **An Initial Call**

God is in the business of giving out assignments, tasks, adventures, partnerships, or whatever you want to label them. It is simply His calling. The call came to Abraham, Moses, Joshua, Caleb, Rahab, and to you and me. How often do His callings involve easy assignments? Never! This shows that God does not put a high premium on comfortable lives. (Comfort will come in heaven.) My calling is to do God's bidding with the people I love as Pastor of Trinity Church with a mission to build fully devoted followers of Christ on the Northshore of New Orleans in the midst of the greatest natural disaster in the history of the United States. **I didn't choose this. God called. What is your calling?**

2. **Our Response**

When God calls, normally people don't say, *"God, will you super-size my call?"* Normally the response includes some measure of fear — fear of failure, inadequacy, etc. Wasn't that the case with the 10 spies who wanted to go back to Egypt because there were giants in the land? Moses, as well, had plenty of excuses when God asked him to go to the most powerful man on the planet and say, *"I want to take your labor force."* There are days that I have felt the same. I am well aware of our giants. Some days I ask, *"Am I crazy? Will I survive?"* It seems overwhelming some days with four staff short, shepherding hurting people, preparing the launch of a new children's building, juggling a financially complex time of capital campaign and furnishings for ministry, running teams, holding together a ministry that has so many families moving out of the area, running Pastor SEARCH teams, and trying to strategically reinvent the ministry. **How about you? Have you got any giants like I have?** Who is saying, *"It's not possible. We've never done it that way before. I won't let you. Let's go back to Egypt."*?

3. Assurance

Fortunately, God never says to fearful people, *"Never mind."* He gives assurance. The #1 command in scripture is *"Fear not"* (366 times) and often the words *"for I am with you"* are attached. Joshua was told, *"Be strong and courageous for I am with you."* Paul heard, *"Do not fear, go on speaking, do not be silent, I am with you."* The Psalmist said, *"Yea, though I walk through the valley of the shadow of death, I will fear no evil, for Thou art with me."* I can't tell you the encouragement of God's tender assurances that come daily through His Word, prayer, God sightings, people, and His still small voice. **Whatever you struggle with today, Jesus knows your name and your need, and He is able.**

4. Decision Component

Life often reduces down to a decision point of Faith or Fear. Faith? or Fear? Do you know what I mean? Moses had to decide whether or not to step into the Red Sea, and Joshua experienced the same decision at the Jordan. Would Caleb take the hill country controlled by the giants? At Trinity we have to decide daily if we want to go back to being a nice, comfortable suburban church or will we fulfill our calling in this, our generation. Last night someone said, *"You aren't the church of the stained carpet, but the church of the smelly socks."* Daily we have a choice — Faith or Fear. By faith, we are choosing to bet the farm on God. At times we shake on the Rock, but the Rock does not shake under us. **Are there any "amens" out there?** Let me ask you, *"What would you do — build, launch, give, start, or stop — if fear were not holding you back? Where is God prompting you to launch out? Where do you need to bet the farm on God?"* God plays no FAVORites, only FAITHorites. By the way, if you find yourself doubting and are asking *"How can I have more faith?"* the answer isn't to try harder or to beat yourself up. Think of the solution this way:

Suppose someone said to you, *"I find myself doubting Old Faithful in Yellowstone National Park. I'm not sure Old Faithful can be trusted."* Your advice wouldn't be *"Just try harder,"* but rather, *"Just hang out with Old Faithful. Get to know Old Faithful."* And because Old Faithful is faithful, the better you know it, the more you trust it. The same is true with God. **The key isn't to muster up our own faith, but to get to know God better. Since God is faithful, the more you know Him, the more you will trust Him.**

5. Changed Life

Every time someone says *"Yes"* to God, there is life change … courage gets a little deeper, joy gets a little broader, and you find Jesus is so amazing, sufficient, surprising, and irresistible. There is no one like Jesus. He is so approachable … refreshing … countercultural … and so controversial. As you give your life away, you find life. This is what I see in Trinity people and teams all the time. I see those who are stepping out in faith are having their lives turned upside down. They are alive and living the adventure. I see it with my eyes every day.

I love the example of Henrietta Mears, who had an amazing ministry as Christian Education director at Hollywood Presbyterian Church in Hollywood, California, in the 1930s - 1960s. She was one who mentored and influenced Bill Bright (Campus Crusade for Christ), Dick Halverson (Chaplain of the U.S. Senate), Roy Rogers and Dale Evans, and Billy Graham. It was said that 500 men went into the ministry because of Miss Mears. At one time she was so frustrated there was no good Christian material to use in church that she started Gospel Light publishing house. She thought her region needed a retreat center in the San Bernardino Mountains. She found a plot of land and believed God for the money. She had none. God provided. At the end of her extraordinary life, people asked Miss Mears, *"What would you do different in your life if you had it to do all over again?"* She said, *"I would trust Christ for more!"* I love it. **Let's live that way.**

Pray for us as we bet the farm on God. We are trusting God for the following critical areas:

1. Over half of the Compassion leadership team will be leaving next week. These have been one-to-three-month volunteers. Pray for long-term volunteers. These are critical. Can you give us one month? Three? Six? A year? Is God calling you? This is critical. **Pray!**

2. Pray for four new staff for Trinity Church. We have a potential candidate coming in this weekend for the Associate position. I have extended an offer for one of our other positions. **Pray.**

3. Pray for a strategy meeting with John Gerhardt and Castle Rock on Monday and with Jim Snyder and the EFCA Compassion team the next week. **Our partnerships matter!**

4. Pray for our new building opportunities and renovations. There are so many open doors. **We are going to have to mobilize the entire church to get the building ready.** The builder will be out by April 16, and our Grand Opening for the community is scheduled for June 4.

5. Pray the God of all provisions gives us wisdom how to provide for our ministry. **This is the most strategic**

time we have ever had to reach our community! Pray for people to give generously.

6. **Pray for revival, renewal, revitalization, and for Jesus to be lifted up!**

Betting the Farm on God,

Michael

MARCH 29 **A Financial Request and More Stories of Grace**

I have never been a fundraiser and perhaps never will be. I don't know that I ever want to be a fundraiser. I am simply a pastor of a local church, in the middle of the finest movement of the Spirit of God that I have ever seen. One of my dear friends, and now colleagues in ministry, is raising support to provide for his family to continue to help lead the work of outreach here in the Gulf Region. I am referring to Mark Lewis, our crisis response director for EFCA-Compassion. If you have been to Trinity, you know Mark as our Field General, mastermind of the operation, and the man who loves Christ and teams.

Mark and his wife Denise were faithfully serving Jesus in Pennsylvania when Katrina hit. Mark was an engineer and Denise, a stay-at-home mom with their three wonderful kids. Mark called Jim Snyder of Compassion Ministry and was told, *"I need someone in Louisiana tomorrow."* Mark's one-week trip to Louisiana turned into a long-term, life changing opportunity!

Mark and Denise's passion to help people impacted by disasters had been growing for some time. Since 1993, this couple has participated in crisis response ministry following floods in the Midwest, Pennsylvania, and West Virginia; an earthquake in Turkey; a devastating tornado in Campbelltown, Pennsylvania; Hurricane Ivan; and now Hurricane Katrina. For an equally long time, they prayed for the EFCA to start a crisis response ministry. In fact, Denise wrote an undergraduate thesis on this very topic in 2000!

I can tell you the call of God is upon their lives. They are choice players in the Kingdom and are bearing incredible fruit. In Luke 16: 1 - 10 Jesus tells a story about how the children of light should practice shrewdness with money in accomplishing Kingdom exploits:

"Now He was also saying to the disciples, 'There was a certain rich man who had a manager, and this manager was reported to him as squandering his possessions. And he called him and said to him, "What is this I hear about you? Give an account of your management, for you can no longer be manager." And the manager said to himself, "What shall I do, since my master is taking the management away from me? I am not strong enough to dig; I am ashamed to beg. I know what I shall do, so that when I am removed from the management, people will welcome me into their homes." And he summoned each one of his master's debtors, and he began saying to the first, "How much more do you owe my master?" And he said, "A hundred measures of oil."And he said to him, "Take your bill, and sit down quickly and write fifty." Then he said to another, "And how much do you owe?"And he said, "A hundred measures of wheat." He said to him, "Take your bill, and write eighty." And his master praised the unrighteous manager because he had acted shrewdly; for the sons of this age are more shrewd in relation to their own kind than the sons of light. And I say to you, make friends for yourselves by means of the wealth of unrighteousness, that when it fails, they will receive you into the eternal dwellings. He who is faithful in a very little thing is faithful also in much; and he who is unrighteous in a very little thing is unrighteous also in much.' "

I cannot think of an investment that has greater Kingdom potential than strategically investing in helping Mark and Denise Lewis get up to full missionary support. They are currently at 25% support. Would you pray about this opportunity? If you are associated with a church with a missions committee, would you ask them about the possibility of the church adopting the Lewis family?

Stories:

I continue to be amazed by the life change that the Holy Spirit is doing in the lives of team members:

1. Tonight, I had dinner with a 24-year-old long-term volunteer. He told me that the Lord has been speaking into his heart these words, *"Take it home with you."* This is a recurring message that is supernaturally being impressed upon teams — that the tangible expression of the love of Christ practiced here can be a way of life back home.

2. One church has had 20% of their church come on work teams so far. This short-term experience is revolutionizing hearts and strategies back home as God is giving incredible energy and ideas for "compassion ministry" in their own backyard.

3. Many teams are returning home and starting "compassion ministry" in their churches. They simply assemble teams who go out in Jesus's name and help people in their own personal "Katrinas." In so doing, God often opens up doors for the gospel. How simple! How biblical! **How compelling!**

4. A woman approaching 70 said, *"I have never been on a mission trip my whole life"* (until last week). Her woman's group raised money to send her. She brought plenty of Vicoden and Ben-Gay. She made an outstanding contribution to our food services ministry. You should have seen her smile! **How compelling!**

5. One team went to Wal-Mart. It was closed, but they discovered the night security man. This 24-year-old was reading Acts but didn't understand what he was reading. (This reminds me of Philip and the Ethiopian in Acts 8.) They helped him understand Jesus and invited him to Trinity. **How compelling!**

6. In our service on Sunday, we showed pictures of a home destroyed by Katrina and then rebuilt by teams.

The best thing was, the couple who lived there has joined Trinity Church and stood to meet the church body. Tears flowed throughout the Worship Center.

7. One woman who came with a team in October prayed and prayed that the lessons learned at Trinity could be transferred to her community back home. This included ministering to those involved in drugs, gangs, fights, etc. Back home she started practicing Servant Evangelism Outreach. She paid the price … God prepared her … She prayed dangerously … God pried everything out of her hands so that there was nothing left … except Him. Yet, God worked miracles in the church, and part of a closed down mall was given to them to extend the works of compassion — rent-free!

8. Last week we sent out teams from Trinity. 130 people strong, mostly college students on spring break, were sent out into the area to work. Someone in the community commented, *"You people are everywhere."*

9. A team member bumped into a man at Home Depot who had roof damage from the hurricane. The team member suggested that maybe his team could come over and repair it for him for free. The man in the store said, *"That won't be necessary. A team from Trinity Church is coming over in the morning to fix the roof."* **Christians on teams are everywhere!**

10. One man came down with a work team in January. While gutting a home, he felt God challenging him to make himself available to Him for whatever He calls him to do. He went back home, and God called him to run for City Council in his hometown of 50,000, a suburb of St. Louis, Missouri. He says, *"Some days, I am scared to death."* Yet, he is stepping out in faith. Pray for him. The vote is on April 4. **Wow!**

Please pray. It makes the difference in the work of God.

1. Pray for us as we hire a follow-up director and a pastor of adult ministry. It looks like God is providing.

2. Pray for us to discover who is to lead our Children's Ministry. Pray for a pastor/director. We are in need of leads and God's direction.

3. Pray for us as we near completion of our Family Discipleship Center. It's getting close! The contractor will be done by April 16. The grand opening for the community is June 4. Pray for planning, provision, and outreach potential.

4. Pray for my son Jonathan as he finishes up his first year at Baylor University. It is a big transition from high school to college. Pray Jonathan discovers God's vocational calling in God's perfect time.

5. Pray for wisdom on whether I should write a book about what God is doing here. Many are suggesting this. Is this God's will? Do I have time? How big a priority is this?

Betting the Farm on God,

Michael

APRIL 7 **Calling All Prayer Warriors**

Over the last six months, I have feasted upon and been sustained by the God of Exodus 17. The people of God faced a great challenge in their confrontation with the Amalekites. Joshua and the men engaged them while Moses went up to the hilltop to raise his hands in dependence upon God. Oh, how he must have prayed. While his hands were raised, the battle went well. When his arms drooped, the mission was hindered, and the enemy made inroads. Two friends came to his rescue and lifted his arms. The victory was secured.

Here in Covington our arms often droop. We covet your prayers. Prayer is the battle because the prevailing power of God flows through prayer. Prayer turns the tide. Prayer is *"the slender nerve that moves the Arm of Omnipotence"* (Charles Spurgeon). It's such a mystery, but God works through praying people. Prayer accomplishes what hard work, tenacity, and strategy can't. I wonder how much money has been given, lives have been changed, people saved, hearts softened, and territory taken from the evil one because believers have undergirded us in prayer. **Please don't forget to pray.**

Prayer requests for Trinity Church:

1. Pray for the unprecedented opportunity to reach our community for Christ. Ask God for boldness, courage, and wisdom in reaching out to a needy people who hunger for hope.

2. Pray for church members who are attempting to re-emerge from disaster. Many have no discretionary time and are stressed. Children, too! Pray for strains on marriages. Pray for many warriors who serve others above themselves.

3. Pray for a weary staff. Being four staff short causes all to do double and triple duty. Pray for strength, endurance, and patience.

4. Praise God that candidates are on the horizon to fill these positions:

   a. Stephen Lay from Dallas Seminary will be candidating this Sunday for the pastor of adult ministry position.

   b. Becky McLain chose to accept the position for follow-up ministry.

c. Fred Hoffman has become our bookkeeper and probably our administrator.

d. We have some wonderful candidates now for the children's pastor.

5. Pray for the completion of our new children's building. The construction company will move out in a couple of weeks. The entire church needs to be mobilized to finish turning the shell into a home by May 13.

6. Pray for the grand opening during the month of June when we invite the Northshore community to visit with us. Each Sunday will include a major children's event including storytellers, puppets, ventriloquist, "Commandos" (they break bricks, tear phone books, etc.), balloons, prizes, picnics, etc. These celebrations will enable families in the community to check out what God has provided. Our desire is to connect people to Jesus and a local church so that moms and dads can be supported and children can have one of the best hours of their entire week. Our focus is on discipleship and evangelism. Our mission is to develop fully devoted followers of Christ.

7. Pray for laborers to work with our massive workdays and for an expanded army of volunteers to work with every aspect of children's ministry.

8. Pray for resources to continue to serve Jesus. Katrina has brought about uncertain times. Pray for $50,000 needed for furnishings. Our capital campaign fund for our new building has been greatly hampered by Katrina. We are praying for wisdom in how to handle this and the provision of over a half million dollars.

9. Pray for preaching messages coming over the next four months.

a. Two weeks will focus on our vision for Trinity and Compassion.

b. The week after Easter will be on "Decoding the *DaVinci Code*."

c. I will then begin preaching a series going through The Book of Luke and looking at Jesus. My favorite person to preach on! In fact, if you want to get to know God — look at Jesus.

10. Pray for our continued interaction with teams — 130 were here last week, and more have come this week. These are choice people. Pray for clarification of our mission, depth in our partnerships, money to not grind to a halt, and wisdom that will allow for longevity.

Here is a letter that illustrates the continued work:

Dear Michael,

I just want to encourage you and the church with a brief testimony from a couple in Chalmette. When we arrived, I asked the owner as to how he was doing. He replied, "Before Katrina, I was worth two million dollars. Today I am worth nothing. I wish I was dead."

I was about to say, "Don't be afraid, the Lord sees you." Instead, I said, "We're here to help you. It's going to be okay." Later that day, three more groups showed up to work on his house (about 35 people) plus the "wiener wagon." The owner could not believe that so many people cared for him and his family. Later that day, we prayed as a group, and the owner prayed, "Help me, Lord, with my unbelief. Give me faith to believe."

Sometimes, Mike, people have to see the Lord before they can hear Him. And sometimes it takes a whole church. The scriptures encourage us "to let our light shine that people may see our good works." The church's efforts and outreach for many Katrina households have been nothing less than a miracle.

Mike, the Lord sees the church's efforts and hearts to come alongside and be the hands and feet of Jesus joining churches throughout the nation and the globe to step into their boats, as to say (Mark 6: 51), to give grace through works to the people of Louisiana, for it is in the church's efforts the Lord is able to calm their storm and calm the seas and the winds that tear their faith and hearts, that they may believe. Keep up the good work of sowing seed for the Kingdom. He loves you. The Lord is faithful and there to amaze. Take courage. He sees your efforts. Don't forget the loaves.

A word for the church; share it joyfully. The Lord is our Shepherd.

A brother that cares

Thank you, dear friends, for prayer. I asked a friend this week, *"Am I crazy for being involved in all we've got going on?"* Without your prayers I would be in a heap, buried, undone, and ruined. The job is so massive, yet Jesus is so able. It is amazing what He continues to do through weak, limited, frail people like us who make things up one day at a time. Keep praying for us semi-cracked vessels who desire deeply to be poured out for him. Our hearts register deeply with this passage:

"Therefore, since we have this ministry, as we received mercy, we do not lose heart, but we have renounced the things hidden because of shame, not walking in craftiness or adulterating the word of God, but by the manifestation of truth commending ourselves to every man's conscience in the sight of God. And even if our gospel is veiled, it is veiled to those who are perishing, in whose case the god of this world has blinded the minds of the unbelieving so that they might not see the light of the gospel of the glory of Christ, Who is the Image of God. For we do not preach ourselves but Christ Jesus as Lord, and ourselves as your bond servants for Jesus's sake. For God, Who said, 'Light shall shine out of darkness,' is the One Who has shone in our hearts to give the Light of the knowledge of the glory of God in the face of Christ. But we have this treasure in earthen vessels, so that the surpassing greatness of the power will be of God and not from ourselves; we are afflicted in every way, but not crushed; perplexed, but not despairing; persecuted, but not

forsaken; struck down, but not destroyed; always carrying about in the body the dying of Jesus, so that the life of Jesus also may be manifested in our body. For we who live are constantly being delivered over to death for Jesus's sake, so that the life of Jesus also may be manifested in our mortal flesh. So death works in us, but life in you."

— 2 Corinthians 4: 1 - 12

Betting the Farm on God,

Michael

APRIL 22 ***You're Not Crazy!***

You're not crazy! These are words our teams need to hear. Our team volunteers have now exceeded 2,700 and have logged in 110,000 man hours. There were 142 last week. **Wow!**

Over the past several weeks, the volunteers have included a high percentage of college students. Some of these students have given up the beaches of Florida for New Orleans. They gave up fun in the sun to gut homes. Narcissism has given way to activism. These young adults are about the cause of Christ. They are not crazy! I am so encouraged by hundreds of college students.

Our volunteers have given up vacations to be in the devastated Gulf Coast. Often they drive across the country, sleeping a night or two in a church basement or a Motel 6. At Trinity, they sleep on a stained carpet on the floor with 80 others and choose to work all day in the heat. They get back to Trinity tired and drenched with sweat. **Yet, they are not crazy!**

Volunteers constantly tell me that their lives are turned upside down. In losing their life, they find life. In giving, they receive. In dying, they find they are really living ... some more than they ever have in their entire lives. These volunteers are making a difference. Beauty is coming out of ashes. Where sorrow resided at night, joy is coming in the morning. Our volunteers are not crazy!

Our Wednesday night services have been electrifying lately. A week ago, it seemed that every team brought their worksite homeowner to the service. Imagine — broken, devastated people who lost virtually everything. Yet, an army of volunteers had been with them for the week. Volunteers and homeowners stood to their feet and exclaimed joy, hope, and thankfulness. The sharing could have gone on all night. These volunteers are not crazy!

One homeowner said, *"Before Katrina, I was worth two million dollars. Now I am worth nothing. I wish I were dead."* A team member thought about saying, *"Don't be afraid. The Lord sees you."* Instead he said, *"We are here to help you."* Thirty-five team members arrived and blew this man away. During a prayer meeting at the end of the day, the homeowner prayed, *"Help me, Lord, with my unbelief. Give me faith to believe."* The team volunteer said, *"Sometimes Mike, people have to see the Lord before they can hear Him."*

One team said, *"The mission of New Orleans has restored PASSION and compassion to the entire congregation of Faith Evangelical Free, Woodruff, Wisconsin."* They are having community events (with local media coverage) to re-tell the stories of what God did in New Orleans. The team needed a truck to get a huge amount of donated bathroom home accessories from Wisconsin to New Orleans. Where would the truck come from? They heard the story of my desperation early in Katrina when I told my associate, *"Go into Covington, look for the first 18-wheel truck driver you see, and tell him that God needs your truck!"* If you remember, God provided the truck in two hours. This team stepped out in faith, called a truck owner, and God provided a truck. God is awesome! *"The eyes of the LORD move to and fro throughout the earth that He may strongly support those whose heart is completely His."*

— 2 Chronicles 16: 9

Amen? Amen.

Pray:

1. Pray for me. I am just keeping my head above water. The opportunities are incredible. However, being short-

staffed is stretching. We are voting on a candidate Sunday and diligently interviewing others. Pray for strength, wisdom, and endurance. Thank God for what He is doing despite our weakness and limitations. God often uses the weak things of this world. He has one weary pastor right now.

2. Pray for our strategic planning this week on the future of our Compassion ministry. This is so important. I believe our souls will be damaged if we get out of the Katrina ministry before God's timing. If we fix up our own homes and neighborhood and then forget about the poor and the city, we will not be about God's heart. Pray for us as we continue our commitment to being the church of the stained carpet for the long run.

3. Pray for resources to continue the work. We need $50,000 for furnishings for our new building and over $500,000 to pay off our new building.

4. Pray for a massive mobilization effort over the next 30 days to prepare our family discipleship building for effective service — self-help, painting, playgrounds, projects, decorations, etc.

5. Pray for our month-long open house for the entire community during the month of June. Our desire is to reach out to the Northshore with the love of Jesus. The community is white unto harvest.

   The June schedule is as follows:

   June 4: Children — Jubilee Gang — high-energy multi-media ministry experience
   Adults — Steven Mosley, one-man drama (Rick Warren's drama pastor)

June 11: Children — Gene Cordova, ventriloquist
Building Dedication / Community Picnic
June 12-16: Vacation Bible School — Mega Sports Camp
June 18: Children — Vacation Bible School Sunday
June 25: Children — Commandos! USA — high-energy
power team imparting God's message

6. Pray for revival in the Gulf region and at Trinity Church.

Betting the Farm on God,

Michael

APRIL 30 **The Jesus Movement**

Lately, I have been asking questions of the early church that might radically influence the Jesus movement today.

1. How did an obscure, marginalized Jesus movement become the dominant faith of the western world in just a few centuries?

2. How did Christ followers convince people they weren't vagabonds, gypsies, or involved in a cult?

3. How did the Christian community in the first century go from being one/one-zillionth of the population to 56% of the Roman Empire? That is a growth rate of 40% per decade!

4. How did they grow so rapidly with no power, soldiers, weapons, or buildings?

5. How did they turn the world upside down in spite of persecution — thrown to the lions in the coliseums, arrests, pressure, and scattering (1 Peter 1: 1). The believers lived in catacombs, pup tents, and caves.

How did they do it? In 1 Peter, I found Christ followers:

"Beloved, I urge you as aliens and strangers to abstain from fleshly lusts which wage war against the soul. Keep your behavior excellent among the Gentiles, so that in the thing in which they slander you as evildoers, they may because of your good deeds, as they observe them, glorify God in the day of visitation." — 1 Peter 2: 11 - 12

I. Lived a New Kind of Life

While the first-century world had long stopped listening to believers, they still watched them. What did they see? Here are a few examples:

A. Rome was a hierarchical society with people divided into rigid classes. Everything reinforced the caste system. Clothes showed what class you were in. I know it's hard to imagine a culture where clothes reflect someone's status, but in the Roman culture, it was true. What happened in the Jesus movement? Masters would serve slaves. Slaves would eat first. Slaves would weep. There was never a community like this.

B. In the ancient world, was it better to be born a boy or a girl? A boy! One historian writes, *"Exposure of unwanted female infants (the practice of just abandoning them until they would die outside somewhere) was legal, morally accepted, widely practiced by all social classes in the Greco-Roman world."*

Here is a letter that I just read this week. It was written during the first century by a Roman husband to his wife. Apparently, she was pregnant. This is what he writes, believing himself to be a good husband:

"Know that I am still in Alexandria. I beg you to take good care of our baby son. If you are delivered of a

child before I come home, if it is a boy, keep it. If it is a girl, discard it. You have sent me word, 'Don't forget me.' How could I forget you? I beg you not to worry."

The Jesus movement came along and treated women differently … valued … treasured … respected, and all life was sacred. Little girls and boys were prized. It is no wonder women flocked to the church.

C. Several times in the early church there were massive epidemics. One wiped out one-quarter of the population of cities in the Roman Empire, and another took one-third. The Roman writer Dionysius says of the fear in the population, *"They pushed sufferers away and fled from their dearest, throwing them into roads before they were dead, and treated unburied corpses as dirt, hoping to avert disease."*

What did Christ followers do?

They took people in. They cared for the sick and dying. They did this sometimes at the cost of their own lives. There was never a community like this. The result was a church of irresistible influence that became a catalyst for change.

Sheldon Vanauken said, *"The best argument for Christianity is Christians; their joy, their certainty, their completeness. But the strongest argument against Christianity is also Christians — when they are somber and joyless, when they are self-righteous and smug in complacent consecration, when they are narrow and repressive, then Christianity dies a thousand deaths."*

II. Did Good Deeds as a Way of Life

"...because of your good deeds, as they observe them, glorify God in the day of visitation."

Isn't this the way of Jesus:

Matthew 5: 16 They may see your good deeds

Luke 6: 31 - 35 Love your enemies, do good to them

Acts 20: 35 It is more blessed to give than to receive

Romans 12: 20 - 21 Overcome evil with good

Galatians 6: 9 - 10 Let us do good to all people

Ephesians 2: 10 Do good works

2 Thessalonians 3: 13 Do not grow weary of doing good

1 Timothy 6: 17 - 19 To do good, to be rich in good deeds

Titus 3: 8 Engage in good deeds

Titus 2: 11 - 14 Eager to do what is good

Hebrews 10: 24 Spur one another on to love and good deeds

1 Peter 3: 13 Eager to do good

III. Did Good Deeds as a Way of Life among Skeptics

Historian Will Durant said this:

"Never had the world seen such a dispensation of alms as was now organized by the Church. ... She helped widows, orphans, the sick or infirm, prisoners, victims of natural catastrophes; and she frequently intervened to protect the lower orders from unusual exploitation or excessive taxation. In many cases, priests gave all their property to the poor ... others devoted fortunes to charitable work. The church or her rich laymen founded public hospitals on a scale never known before.... Pagans admired the steadfastness of Christians in caring for the sick in cities stricken with famine or pestilence."

Isn't this what is needed today? We live in an age of skepticism and cynicism. We say, *"Everyone has an angle"* or *"There is no free lunch."* We think everyone is hyping, selling, or spinning. This is where Christians and good deeds come in. It is by stealthy, radical acts of service that we shock people. These free expressions of compassion don't grab the headlines, but they do change lives. The church of the first century was at its best in the shadows, underground, quiet, humble, yet totally countercultural. You couldn't keep people away. It was what everyone was looking for.

Isn't that true today? Our Kingdom weapons are brooms, rocks, visits, listening ears, open hands, and generous hearts. The church is not just a "religious services provider" whose job is to make sure everyone in the church is happy while everyone else is going to hell. Rather, we gather on Sunday as the body of Christ and then are turned loose on Monday to practice good deeds in the world. Like it or not, we are "living epistles" read by all men. The truth is, *"People don't go where the action is; they go where love is."* Jesus said, *"All men will know you are My disciples by the love you have for one another."* A visual aid prepares the listener to hear the truth. Right?

IV. Shared Their Hope

1 Peter 3: 15 says, *"But sanctify Christ as Lord in your hearts, always being ready to make a defense to everyone who asks you to give an account for the hope that is in you, yet with gentleness and reverence."*

As we live in a new way and practice good deeds, God will open doors. There is the opportunity to share Jesus.

This is the plan that allowed early Christians to turn the world upside down. Jesus is burning it into my heart that this is His plan for our days as well. Let's have at it.

Betting the Farm on God,

Michael

MAY 15 **Cracked Pots for Jesus**

What a difference eight months makes! Back in August, I was gearing up to re-launch our new ministry year with a full staff and a new building right on the horizon. The elders had just unanimously approved my 70-page strategic plan. We were ready to roll. Oh, how the Trinity — the Father, Son and Holy Spirit — must have had fun with my plan of operating from strength. What a good chuckle they had over "Michael's plan." They decided they could do better!

Exceedingly better! Included in the revised plan was their desire to teach me, *"But we have this treasure in earthen vessels, so that the surpassing greatness of the power will be of God and not from ourselves."*

— 2 Corinthians 4: 7

Oh, how I needed to learn that God often uses cracked pots rather than fine china. I can now relate well to Judges 7. Remember the time Israel was invaded and oppressed by the Midianites at harvest time? Year after year rolled along until Gideon raised an army of 32,000. That's a lot of men until you realize the Midian army was as thick as locusts and their camels could no more be counted than the sand on the seashore (7: 12). The enemy army was at 135,000. Gideon's inexperienced troops were outnumbered 4 to 1. God said, *"Gideon, you have a numbers problem."* Gideon was glad God saw this, too. However, God said, *"You have too many troops. Have a troop reduction."* **Wow!** A special waiver was offered to opt out of battle, and 22,000 men opted out. Now Gideon's army was at 10,000, and he was outnumbered 13 to 1. God again said, *"Gideon, you have a numbers problem."* I'm sure Gideon was thinking, *"God, I don't know if I want Your help anymore."* Sure enough, there was another troop reduction from 10,000 to 300. Now they were outnumbered 450 to 1. If you read the text carefully, it appears that the "geeky" guys were left and not the "Navy seals" types. The only guys left were the ones who lapped water like a dog.

Isn't this God? Often when He does something big, He stacks the odds against Himself so the credit will go to Him alone. Gideon and his 300 were stripped of everything and needed to learn to depend totally on God or perish. They were learning a God-confidence based upon His sufficiency rather than self-confidence.

God's promise, *"This can be nothing other than the sword of Gideon. God has given the Midianites and the whole camp into our hands. Arise."* (7: 14 - 15a paraphrased). Their God-confidence oozed. The 300 were divided into three companies of 100. Weapons were issued — trumpets (rams' horns), clay pots, and torches to hide in the pots. In the darkness of the night, they circled the Midianite camp. Suddenly, 300 clay pots smashed, 300 torches pierced the night, 300 rams' horns blared, and 300 voices shouted, *"The sword of the Lord and of Gideon."* Panic seized the Midianites as they stumbled out of bed. Confusion reigned, and many were trampled. All fled! The truth: The power is not in the clay pot, but in the One who resides in the jar! **In the midst of the brokenness of the cracked pot, the light of God shines brightest.**

I'm learning that God often uses weak, broken pottery and seldom uses fine china. Rather than operating from my plan of strength, God wanted me to learn His sufficiency in the midst of weakness. He stripped away my props quickly:

Empty nest
- Evacuation
  - House damage/trees down
    - House unlivable
      - Church scattered
        - No offerings
          - Hurting people
          - 30% of church gone
        - Building program
      - New building pledge system collapse
    - Postpone fall furnishings campaign
  - Parents' move
- Four staff positions short

Elder board changes

God took away the props and stripped away some encumbrances — man-made securities, self-reliance, and self-effort. He took me through the Refiner's fire and pruned the dead wood because He insists our spiritual life and strength come not from our sufficiency but His.

I am not who I used to be. I'm lighter and realize I am alive in the cause of Christ. Jesus always makes a way that includes streams in the wilderness, beauty out of ashes, life out of death, and joy after sorrow. *"For me, to live is Christ."* —Philippians 1:21a

How beautiful was Sunday morning as worship tables displayed cracked pots and candles lit. Each one who attended was equipped with a flashlight. At one point we turned off the lights, and I asked Trinity folks a series of questions:

1. If you've experienced "desert times" and seen God faithful, turn your light on.
2. If you've had job loss or job troubles, yet today you are working, turn your light on.
3. If burdens were crushing you this year, and you couldn't carry them on your own, yet He carried you, and you are still in the game of life, turn your light on.
4. If you have become a Christian this year, or rededicated your life to Him, turn your light on.
5. If you've had a major financial blessing, turn your light on.
6. If you are weak but know He is strong, turn your light on.
7. If God has used you over the last eight months, turn your light on.
8. If you identify with cracked pots imagery, yet know the power is not the pot, but the One in the pot, turn your light on.

You should have seen the hundreds of little lights that were shining in darkness Sunday illustrating the sufficiency of Jesus. **Hallelujah! Amen.**

Praise & Prayer:

1. Praise: One man said, *"I wondered why I was coming (to church), now I don't want to leave."*

2. Teams still pour in weekly, though two weeks ago the Compassion staff had their first "down" week since Katrina hit. They deserved the rest. Pray for Mark, Jenn, and all of the team.

3. Pray for the wonderful teams — A man who was committed to coming injured his hand and was not even able to open a Bible. He told a team member he thought he broke his hand, and his New Orleans visit was questionable. The entire team found out andasked the church to pray. That night, while getting up in the middle of the night, he tripped on the bone of his 125-lb. dog and fell down onto his hand and heard a big pop. He moved his hand and found it was all better. Canine Chiropractics or Divine Provision? The man served in New Orleans all week.

   A lawyer, back for the second time, commented how he finds life so different in the midst of disaster response. People operate out of being at the same level as servants rather than a hierarchy. He finds that to be a display of what heaven will be like.

4. Pray for a million details in finishing our new Family Discipleship Center in preparation for our four weeks of grand opening during the month of June. There is still a lot to do, and the construction company is not finished yet.

Betting the Farm on God,

Michael

JUNE 1 **Acts 29 Stories and Urgent Prayer Requests**

If you have been to Trinity on a team, you know that sharing nights can be sooo good. There is nothing like recounting the deeds of the Lord! Tuesday night was one of the best. The stories of God are still being written. It's like Acts 29!

Stories:

1. Becky from Pennsylvania has been here four times to help! One of the things she learned from a previous visit was to *"take this home with you."* At home, she bumped into a woman in K-Mart who was walking around in a daze. Her home had burned down the night before. She had no money and needed a ride home. But, she also needed a booster seat for her child. Becky bought the woman a booster seat and took her and her three children to the motel where they were staying. The woman said, *"No one has ever been so nice to me."*

2. A team of eight came from Grace Community Church in Maryland to spend the week following up on people that Trinity has reached out to in the past. An 86-year-old Louisiana woman had previously had three or four teams help her at her house. One hundred ninety-five trees had been taken off her property, and her yard still looked like a war zone. This new team visited her, and she assumed that, since the services were provided, it was now time to pay up.

   They said, *"We do not want your money. We are here for the love of Christ, representing Trinity Church. Trinity Church wants to love this area, and cover it with the love of Jesus."* They talked about her relationship with Jesus Christ. This team volunteer said, *"I have been studying the Bible for 28 years. I have never heard a community talk about the church like we were in the first century ... talking about Christians because they love so much ... people talking about Trinity Church. 'Oh, those people from Trinity' ... good rumors."*

3. A lady named Jessie visited a person who lived with all kinds of Confederate flags surrounding his home.

(Jessie is a beautiful, zealous Christian black woman.) When she saw all of this, God whispered, *"I'm in charge of this, not you."* The man at the house came out with a long beard, a pony tail, jeans, a wife-beater t-shirt, and a Confederate belt buckle. God whispered, *"This is all about Me."* What a conversation it was! Jessie and the man were both from the south. The man had had two heart attacks and couldn't take care of his roof. Trinity fixed it for him. Jessie and her partner prayed for this man and left a Bible and a Wal-Mart gift card. He welcomed them to return and then said to Jessie, *"Can I give you a hug before you leave?"* God worked! **Jesus tears down walls.**

4. Angie from Oklahoma attends Oklahoma Fellowship E-Free Church. Before coming, her team went through an evangelism class. Upon arrival, Angie volunteered for kitchen duty. On Tuesday, during the day, a young woman from New Orleans came into the church. God whispered to Angie, *"Has someone shared the gospel with her? Someone should share the gospel with her. Are you going to share the gospel with her?"* Now the only other time Angie tried to share the gospel with someone, the person wasn't interested. This time, the woman trusted Christ!

Prayer Requests:

1. June 4, 11, 18 and 25 is our big open house to the community for our new Family Discipleship Center. 15,000 square feet of space will be used for Great Commission enterprises. The community has been invited through 10,000 mailers, newspaper ads, and personal invitations. Pray for the salvation of many and the possibility of connecting unchurched families to Trinity.

2. Pray for hundreds of details that need to be completed in finishing the building by Sunday. We are running out of hours.

3. The schedule for June is as follows:
June 4: Children — Jubilee Gang — high-energy multi-media ministry experience
Adults — Steven Mosley, one-man drama (Rick Warren's drama pastor)
June 11: Children — Gene Cordova, ventriloquist
Building Dedication / Community Picnic
June 12-16: Vacation Bible School — Mega Sports Camp
June 18: Children — Vacation Bible School Sunday
June 25: Children — Commandos! USA — high-energy power team imparting God's message

4. Pray that we find the right children's pastor. The search continues. We have added two of the four staff needs, one is on the way (pray for the sale of a house), and the children's pastor is still in process.

Thank you for praying. We have worked for three+ years for this grand opening. **May Jesus be honored!**

Betting the Farm on God,

Michael

JUNE 21 **Basketball/Katrina/Michael/Glory to God**

Many of you know that my favorite sport is basketball. I'm cheering for Shaq and the Heat this week in the NBA finals but have already experienced the thrill of the game myself. Jesus is visibly at work on the Northshore of New Orleans as well as the basketball court. For several years now I have been on a basketball team that takes the sport seriously — sometimes too seriously. I play with some great guys from the community, but our team is notorious in the league. We lead the league in technical fouls. One time one of our guys wanted to beat up an opponent in the parking lot after the game. The guy he wanted to punch out was a guy in my church. I walked out to the car with the guy to help protect him. Another time, things got so out of hand that the referee called both teams to mid-court and chewed us out and threatened to toss everyone out of the gym. I could almost see the heading, *"Local Pastor Arrested in Basketball Brawl."* I've wondered, *"Should I stick with this or give it up?"* A delight in the game — and hope for these guys — compelled me to continue. Over time, I have been able to share with each one.

A couple of months ago, to my surprise, one of my teammates showed up at Trinity. After the service I met with him, and he trusted Jesus. **Wow!** He has been at Trinity with his wife and eight (yes, eight) kids ever since. He is growing and hungry for God's Word. Last week he took a week of vacation from his job to be a basketball coach at Vacation Bible School. Kids got saved in his group. He brainstormed with our VBS director about how we could start a monthly basketball camp for fifth-through-ninth grades. It is in the works.

In our new building before the vinyl flooring was laid, we wrote on the floor the names of people we wanted to see saved and occupying our new facility. On that special day, I remember praying for our community and my basketball guys. I'm amazed! The gospel is the power of God unto salvation to all who believe. **I can't wait to see what God will do next!**

Praise:

1. Thanks for praying for our grand opening of the new Family Discipleship Center. The month of "open house" has gone so well. Lots of visitors! Twenty-something kids trusted Jesus as Savior.

   This Sunday we have a power team coming in from Katy, Texas, to share the scripture with the kids. These "Commandos" for Jesus will break books, tear phone books in two, rappel from heights, and share their stories. The furniture for the building seems to arrive daily, and the grass was laid today. I thank God for the gift of this special building. Our desire is to use it to *"help people become fully devoted followers of Jesus Christ."*

2. I continue to thank God for our teams. We have 100 more volunteers this week — Choice people! One couple last week celebrated their 25th wedding anniversary. They had the option of going on a cruise or working here all week, gutting houses and talking to people about Christ. This dear couple chose to join us. Thank you, Chris and Sue Hart, for your compelling devotion to the Savior.

3. Churches continue to send teams and practice great creativity in resourcing the ministry. One church got a donation of two trucks of hats and had a "hat sale" to raise money to continue the work with Compassion. Another woman just donated a trailer and raised $4,000 from her hometown to give to Compassion to go along with the trailer. **Praise the Lord!**

Thank you for not forgetting us. We truly are partners with people in 36 states and six countries. **What a display of the body of Christ.**

Betting the Farm on God,

Michael

P. S. Pray for the rest of the guys on my basketball team. I'll keep you posted!

July 24 **Incredible Teams: God's Choice Players**

My apologies for not writing much lately. I am just trying to keep up. This week, a pastor was trying to call me and located my number in a directory. Unbeknownst to me, two of the digits of the phone number had been transposed. When he called and asked for me, he discovered the number was to a psychiatric ward. He told the nurse *"sorry"* but commented that I probably felt like I needed to be there at times. Pray for strength, wisdom, endurance, and rest.

Having just had our 5,000th volunteer has caused me to be filled with incredible gratitude. 5,000! **That's God at work! 5,000 choice, wonderful servants.** The stories are endless ... Acts 29. Let me convey a few stories that I recall from the last few days:

1. A woman named Janice, who was unemployed, wondered, *"Should I go?"* She was so nervous about New Orleans. The night before the team was leaving, God seemed to say, *"You need to go and help those people."* After ministering, she said, *"Now it has changed my life!"* In fact, Janice took her first steps to quit smoking this week. We rejoiced with her.

2. Two team members trusted Christ last week. **Glory to God.**

3. One man commented this morning that he had never seen a building being used so much for God. We really are the church of the stained carpet. In fact, he made an interesting request. He asked that when we eventually replace the carpet, he would like a piece of the stained carpet to place in his trophy case. **A trophy of Grace!**

4. A New York team has pow-wowed for some time now to impact their community. During their week here, they experienced the open doors that come from "serving evangelism." While working at a house, they talked to homeowners, mailman, mother, uncle, the niece, and others. Servanthood opened the door. They worked with people and become part of them.

5. One woman talked to God about ministry and helping our community. She felt God said, *"No, if I wanted New Orleans fixed, I could fix it. If I didn't want this to happen, it wouldn't have happened. You are not doing this for Me, I'm doing this for you."* Teams continue to talk about God's transformation of teams.

6. A Nebraska team told about their church receiving a significant trust five years ago. They struggled on what to do with the money. Finally, they decided to put it into people and chose to put the money into sending teams to New Orleans. Their challenge has been to practice 1 John 3:18, *"Little children, let us not love with word or with tongue, but in deed and truth."* **Thank you, God.**

7. One team has found itself almost daily getting food and other things from Wal-Mart. They have an interesting approach to reaching out. They bring a Bible with them into Wal-Mart. While waiting in the check-out line, one of the team members discovers the name of the cashier and uses the wait time to write the person's name and a note in the front of the Bible. When it is check-out time, they place the Bible on the conveyer belt along with the rest of their goods. The cashier tries to scan the Bible a couple of times, and then asks, *"Is this your personal Bible?"* The answer is *"No, it's yours."* The team member then presents the Bible to the cashier and shows them their name in the front. Every Bible has been received with delight and astonishment.

I'll stop here. More stories to come.

Betting the Farm on God,

Michael

Editor's Note:

God's response to disaster in New Orleans will continue long after this book is printed. It is our desire that He use its publication to further the efforts He has begun through Trinity Evangelical Free Church, Covington, Louisiana.

All proceeds beyond costs will be folded back into the Compassion effort in the New Orleans and Northshore community.

May God richly bless His servant Michael Sprague and the workers He has sent to assist this brother in fulfilling His purpose.

And may God use *Stories from Katrinaland* to inspire His Church and prosper her mission as His bride.

Pam Reed

In the final weeks before opening,
Trinity's Family Discipleship Center
takes shape.

Appendix

Bridge to Life, © 1969 by The Navigators
Used by permission of NavPress, Colorado Springs, CO.

THE **BRIDGE** TO LIFE

Step 1 — God's Love and His plan

God created us in His own image to be His friend and to experience a full life assured of His love, abundant and eternal.

Jesus said, *"...I have come that they may have life, and have it to the full."*
— John 10: 10b

"...we have peace with God through our Lord Jesus Christ."
— Romans 5: 1

Since God planned for us to have peace and abundant life right now, why are most people not having this experience?

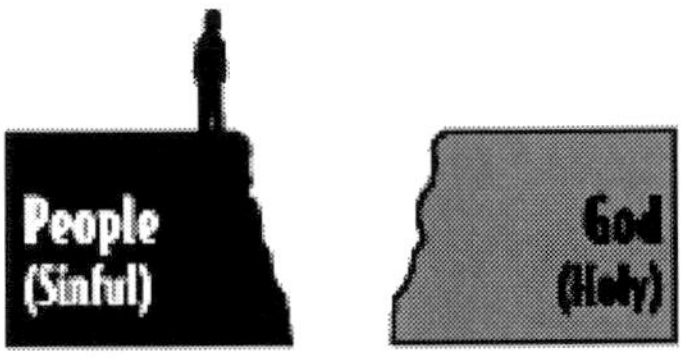

Step 2 — Our Problem: Separation from God

God created us in His own image to have abundant (meaningful) life. He did not make us robots to automatically love and obey Him, but He gave us a will and a freedom of choice.

We chose to disobey God and go our own willful way. We still make this choice today. This results in separation from God.

"For all have sinned and fall short of the glory of God." —Romans 3: 23

"...your iniquities have separated you from your God; your sins have hidden His face from you so that He will not hear." —Isaiah 59: 2

On our own, there's no way we can attain the perfection needed to bridge the gap to God. Through the ages, individuals have tried many ways... without success.

Good works won't do it ... or religion ... or money ... or morality ... or philosophy ...

"There is a way that seems right to a man, but in the end it leads to death." —Proverbs 14: 12

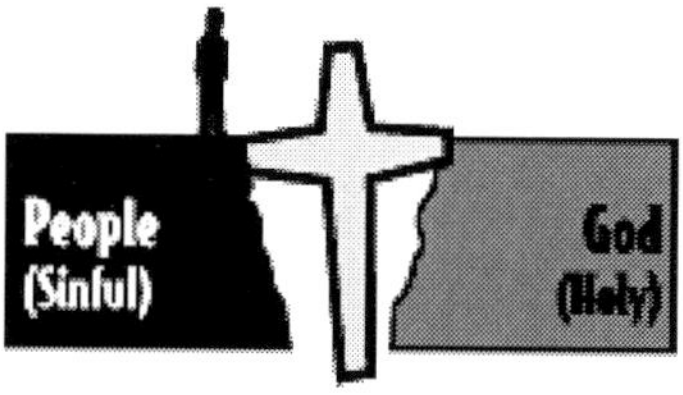

Step 3 — God's Remedy: The Cross

Jesus Christ is the only answer to this problem. He died on the cross and rose from the grave, paying the penalty for our sin and bridging the gap between God and people.

"For Christ died for sins once for all, the righteous for the unrighteous, to bring you to God..." — 1 Peter 3: 18

"For there is one God and one mediator between God and men, the man Jesus Christ." — 1 Timothy 2: 5

"But God demonstrates His own love for us in this: While we were still sinners, Christ died for us." —Romans 5: 8

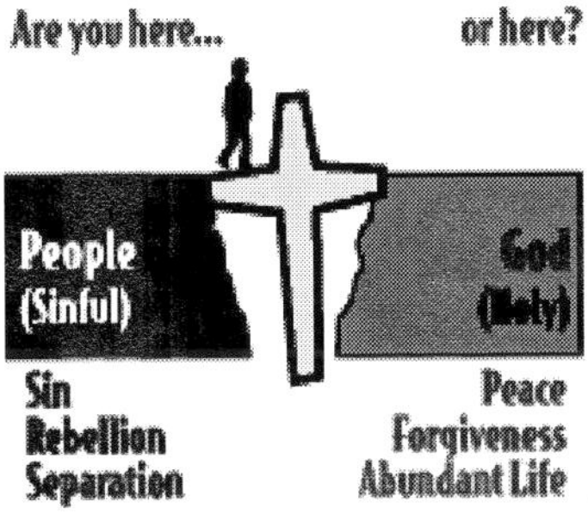

Step 4 — Our Response

Believing means trust and commitment — acknowledging our sinfulness, trusting Christ's forgiveness and letting Him control our life. Eternal, abundant life is a gift for us to receive.

"For God so loved the world that He gave His one and only son, that whoever believes in Him shall not perish but have eternal life."

— John 3: 16

"I tell you the truth, whoever ***hears*** *my word and* ***believes*** *Him Who sent me has eternal life and will not be condemned; he has crossed over from death to life."*

— John 5: 24

Is there any reason why you shouldn't cross over to God's side and be certain of eternal life?

How to receive Christ:

1. Admit your need (I am a sinner).
2. Be willing to turn from your sins (repent).
3. Believe that Jesus Christ died for you on the cross and rose from the grave.
4. Through prayer, invite Jesus Christ to come in and control your life through the Holy Spirit (Receive Him as Lord and Savior of your life).

What to pray:

Dear Lord Jesus,
I know that I am a sinner and need Your forgiveness. I believe that You died for my sins. I want to turn from my sins. I now invite You to come into my heart and life. I want to trust and follow You as the Lord and Savior of my life.

In Your name, Amen.

God's assurance of eternal life

If you've prayed this prayer and are trusting Christ, then the Bible says that you can be sure you have eternal life.

"For, everyone who calls on the name of the Lord will be saved."
— Romans 10: 13

"For it is by grace you have been saved, through faith — and this not from yourselves, it is the gift of God — not by works, so that no one can boast." — Ephesians 2: 8 - 9

"He who has the Son has life; he who does not have the Son of God does not have life. ***I write these things to you who believe in the name of the Son of God so that you may know that you have eternal life."***
— 1 John 5: 12 - 13

Receiving Christ, we are born into God's family through the supernatural work of the Holy Spirit Who indwells every believer...this is called regeneration or the "new birth."

What next?

This is just the beginning of a wonderful new life in Christ.

To deepen this relationship you should:

1. Maintain regular intake of the Bible to know Christ better.

2. For more information see the Word Hand illustration.*

3. Talk to God in prayer every day.

4. For more information see the Prayer Hand illustration.*

5. Tell others about your new faith in Christ.

6. For help doing this, use the same illustration that is presented above. The important thing is that you let others know about your new faith in Christ.

7. Worship, fellowship, and serve with other Christians in a church where Christ is preached.

8. As Christ's representative in a needy world, demonstrate your new life by your love and concern for others.

---

* For other illustrations of the Christian faith, see http://www.navigators.org/us/resources/illustrations